THE STY OF THE BLIND PIG

THE STY OF
THE BLIND PIG

THE BOBBS-MERRILL COMPANY, INC.

● ● ● ● ● ● ● ● ●

AND OTHER PLAYS

Phillip Hayes Dean

Indianapolis-New York

The Bobbs-Merrill Company, Inc.
Indianapolis/New York

Book Design By NANCY DALE MULDOON

To the Hayes Women:

Edna
Nanny
Wanabell
Marie
and my mother, Leatha

And to the honorary Hayes Lady,
Aunt Camile

ACKNOWLEDGMENT

To the NEGRO ENSEMBLE COMPANY:
Douglas Ward Turner
Frances Foster
Adolph Caesar
Clarice Taylor
Moses Gunn
Shauneille Perry

Thank you.

CONTENTS

FOREWORD

Every now and then, or perhaps more often than we know, there comes an artist who seems almost out of his time, or the times, although his work is a distinct monument to the period it presents. This is especially true of Black artists in the United States because of the particular and peculiar placement of our history in this country. Black playwrights have been in existence for a long time despite the fact that they were for the most part ignored by the commercial theatre until the late 1960s. In that eruption attention was paid to the younger and newer writers, whose work mirrored the unrest and generated the excitement and anger of the era. This was of course good, because it opened the long overdue doors of recognition to Black writing as well as breathed a vital puff of life that the American theatre had almost managed to extinguish. Critics rejoiced at the vitality of Black plays and at the same time decried the anger, which they pretended not to understand. The battle raged. Times were turbulent; so were the plays. At last the truth of Black life was being told, and the effects were far-reaching for most Black people. "Turned-off" audiences were recaptured and new ones discovered. Black actors could at last identify with the roles they were playing, and someone even got the idea that perhaps a Black director could interpret with more than an objective eye.

During all this there was a persistent nag in the minds of some that in this great "unfolding of Blackness" not all the truth could —or would—be told: it was all happening too fast. After all, how could 200 years of history be revealed in the span of five or six? One thought of parents, grandparents, great-uncles and -aunts who had lived and fought their battles, whose stories were almost legend by now. Almost. Then came Phillip Hayes Dean. Not discovered, because he was always there. Not bursting on the scene, but standing by with his already recorded scenes of a life not long past yet almost gone forever. The memories of a young man who began his observations in the tough urban Midwest, Chicago by name, where he learned how to be rebellious early. In school, in gangs, in the streets, in the projects, in reform school. He learned other things too, like the sweet strength of Black family life, which is all too often pictured as a series of squabbles and scandals.

Living in a household of four generations, he was witness to the life styles of each era, the interactions and relationships of people who are born, live and die under one roof.

His father was a minister, and, like most preachers' children, he hated the imposed sentence of continual churchgoing, but his eyes and ears captured perfectly the essential beauty in the music and ritual of the Black church: The service, the funeral, the prayer meetings and revivals. These memories were focused with absolute clarity in "The Sty of the Blind Pig."

Sometime during his teens the family moved to Pontiac, Michigan, a place Dean recalls as a small town with its heart gone. It held little for him, but the lingering refrain from his urban beginnings did, so New York claimed him as soon as manhood did. He came to be an actor, but his rebellious nature allowed him only to *re*act once he was introduced to the plight of the Black actor of that period. He turned, or rather *re*turned, to writing, intermittently at first, perhaps nudged subconsciously by some rare teacher of the past who had "reckoned that young Phil could be a writer."

In the late 50's he wrote "The Owl Killer," which was done at the Harlem Workshop, with Diana Sands, Mel Stewart, Ernestine McClendon and others in the cast. It was the latter, then an actress, who had introduced the play to the group. This was to be a pattern for the brash young playwright who refused to knock on any door. Another actress-friend, Osceola Archer, took his "This Bird of Dawning Singeth All Night Long" to the Chelsea Theatre, where it was produced by Bob Cafin. A second success was his, but always on the workshop level, because the commercial theatre had not yet opened its eye to the Black story.

Another friend, the Rev. Eugene Monick, then vicar of St. Clements' Church, introduced "This Bird" to the American Place Theatre, which was housed in the church. In 1969 Phil Dean had his first commercial experience. It too was successful, and a production of his TV script "Johnny Ghost" was done on the Boston-based series, "On Being Black." With Cicely Tyson playing the lead, this event brought Dean further into public attention. "The Sty of the Blind Pig," which he had begun in 1964, was completed by this time, and the Actors' Studio workshop staged it. Once again, an actress friend, Frances Foster, presented the work to Douglas Turner Ward, Artistic Director of the Negro Ensemble Company, and the rest is history. Phillip Dean was known and acclaimed by the major press. "Sty" was given several nominations as "Best Play of the Year." Now there are productions of other works due throughout the city.

Currently a teacher of acting, a career he began at the University of Michigan, Phillip Hayes Dean continues his detailed examination of Black family life and the "family play" which he rightly insists is extremely valid despite current assaults to the contrary. "Because," he says, "every character comes from some man or woman."

Thank you, Phil Dean, for opening the eyes of America to the quiet but unrelenting generations of Black warriors who without you might never have had their stories told.

SHAUNEILLE PERRY
New York, 1972

THE STY OF
THE BLIND PIG

The setting of the play is the Warren apartment on the south side of Chicago. The apartment shows a definite French influence, which is in sharp contrast to the furniture—signs written in silver on blue cardboard quoting verses from the Bible; and photographs—some faded black and white, some faded in tinted color, showing black people, marrying, standing in fields, standing with horses, etc. This apartment, like many apartments in this neighborhood, once was upper middle-class white. The whites moved out with the mass immigration of blacks coming up from the South at around the end of the First World War.

Two French doors, one with a broken pane of glass, are placed in the back wall. They lead to the two bedrooms. Another French door is down stage left, separating the kitchen and living room. Two large windows are cut into the right up-stage wall overlooking the street below. The kitchen is modest and seems a bit too large for the utilities placed there.

The time of the play is the period just before the beginning of the civil rights movement. . . .

ACT I ● ● ●

SCENE 1

The lights fade in on WEEDY WARREN, *sitting before the open window in the living room at dusk. She is an old woman, close to seventy, with hard lines carved in her face. She is dressed in a big black hat and black spring coat. As she sits rocking before the window the light of the dusky evening slowly fades into the night. Down the street, from a little storefront church, a choir can be heard backed by the sound of tambourines.*

CHOIR: [*Off stage*]
Father alone knows all about it
Father alone understands why
Cheer up, my mama, walk in the sunshine
You'll understand all by and by . . .

[*There is a knock at the door as the choir fades out.*]

WEEDY: [*Moves to door*] Is that you, Brother . . . ?
DOC: [*From other side of door*] You gonna open the door?

[WEEDY *unlocks door and then returns to her rocker.*]

WEEDY: C'mon in.

[DOC *is a little man in his mid-fifties, dressed in the period of another time. There is something of the clown in him . . . both a tragic and a comic quality. A black derby hat sits on top of his head and spats cover his shoes. From the vest of his lifeless gray suit dangle several miniature toy pistols. He carries a walking stick and wears a pair of gray felt gloves.*]

DOC: What'd you sittin' up here in the dark for?

WEEDY: Cooler. Bulb heats up th' room.

DOC: [*Moves to cupboard*] Hey, Sister . . .

WEEDY: Naw!

DOC: How you gonna naw me before I ask th' question?

WEEDY: Whenever you start that ole "sister" stuff it means you gettin' ready to borrow money. And since I ain't gonna give nobody no money to play th' numbers with the answer is naw. Don't aid an' abet nobody in gamblin'. An' what are you lookin' for?

DOC: Whiskey.

WEEDY: Lawd, I'm just surrounded by whiskey heads. Keep on . . . be done drink your fool self to death.

DOC: [*Pouring himself a drink*] That's what my wife Nora Lee usta say. [*Mimicking Nora Lee*] "Doc Sweet, honey, you gonna keep drinkin' that ole whiskey till it kills you." Told her that I would be drinkin' whiskey when th' railroad tracks was runnin' over her head. [*Fighting off a creeping nostalgia*] Poor woman's been dead now for twenty years. Came home one day to find out that th' woman had laid down an' died like a dog without any warnin' whatsoever.

WEEDY: You sure gonna haffta give an account of all that ole random talk when Jesus gets back here and looks up your record.

DOC: I'm almost sixty an' he ain't made it back here since I been here. I'm beginnin' to think maybe he ain't comin' back. Can't say that I blame him after th' raw deal he got th' last time he was here. [*Takes his tobacco out and rolls himself a cigarette*] Hey, Sister . . .

WEEDY: Will you not beg me, please. After doin' all your big talk I sure ain't gonna give you nothin' now. Always beggin'! Hate a beggar! . . . Just hate 'em. Put me in th' mind of a woman named Polly Walker. "Beggin' Polly" they usta call her . . . 'cause she was all th' time beggin'. Got so folks hated to see beggin' Polly comin' so much they locked their doors at th' mentionin' of her name.

DOC: What'd you savin' for anyway? Don't you know money was made round to roll from one hand to another? Suppose to keep it rollin'. It's people like you that stopped th' rollin' of money and brought on th' depression.

WEEDY: I don't see you rollin' around none.

DOC: Did when I had it. Usta fall down to th' Dew Drop Inn on Beale Street . . . down in Memphis . . .

WEEDY: That's why you ain't got a pot to pee in now or a window to throw it out of . . . sportin' 'em up.

DOC: [*At window*] What th' . . . [*Raises window*] Hey, you chaps. Those damn kids again. Ev'rytime I come over here they jump all over my car. [*Hollering out of window*] Get your butts off my car before I come down there an' locate my stick in th' vicinity of your hind parts.

WEEDY: Will you not holler outta my window!

DOC: I ain't seen nothin' like these chaps in all my born days.

WEEDY: I reckon they ain't seen nothin' like you

	before. Dressed like that . . . drivin' that ole car. Walkin' 'round in th' warm weather with gloves on. Told you men don't wear gloves no more.
DOC:	Second time today somebody mentioned my gloves. [*Removes dream book and pencil from inside coat pocket*]
WEEDY:	Will you please not write your numbers in my house. [*Watches him take gloves off, remove a small bottle from his pocket. Pours a drop or two in his palms, rubbing them together.*] What's that mess?
DOC:	Lucky oil.
WEEDY:	Last month it was incense.
DOC:	Hit for twenty-five dollars, didn't I?
WEEDY:	Burnin' incense in th' Y.M.C.A. Oughta be ashamed of yourself.
DOC:	I ain't though. [*He moves to door.*] You'd better get ready if you want me to drive you to church.
WEEDY:	I'm ready.
DOC:	Then c'mon.
WEEDY:	Tryin' to wait for Alberta to get home. [*Looking out of window*] Lawd, don't reckon somebody done hit her in th' head an' dragged her off into one of these old deserted buildin's.
DOC:	Sounds like some of Mama's ole random talk.
WEEDY:	Mama had second sight.
DOC:	She had second sight, all right. Woman once told me she saw Abraham Lincoln's ghost ridin' a gray mule. . . .
WEEDY:	Maybe she did.
DOC:	If Abraham Lincoln's ghost had nothin' better to do than ride a gray mule on them dark, muddy roads in Mississippi, then they sure shoulda revoked his ghost pass.
WEEDY:	Maybe she done run off like her ole no-good father. That's th' way Gardner

Warren did . . . just walked outta here one evenin'. . . .

DOC: A nonsmoker who went after th' famous pack of cigarettes an' ain't been heard from since. [*Laughs*] Always liked ole Gardner Warren. Usta love to watch that man eat fish. Never saw anything like it in my life. Man would put fish in one side of his mouth, work his lips, an' th' bones would shoot out on th' other side. Yes, sir, it was like watchin' a machine.

[*A key is heard in the door.* ALBERTA *enters. She is a tall, thin-framed woman in her late thirties. She stands straight and rigid as if she is carrying an unseen burden. She is dressed in a simple print dress that hangs loosely from her body. Her hair is thick, a mixture of gray and black. There is a raw quality about her. She is a woman who has never known pleasure. Pleasure in her life has been equated with sin.*]

ALBERTA: Hello, Mama . . . Uncle Doc. [*Snaps on light*] What are you two sitting up here in the dark for? [*Moves to kitchen table and sets down bag of groceries she has brought in with her*]

WEEDY: Waitin' on you.

ALBERTA: Waiting on me for what?

WEEDY: I told you this morning, before you went to work, that Brother would be over here this evenin' to take you to church.

ALBERTA: Didn't you hear me tell you this morning that I wasn't going to church this evening?

WEEDY: Sister Martin is sittin' down at Mount Hope this very minute waitin' on you . . . to give you the information.

THE STY OF THE BLIND PIG | 7

ALBERTA: Did you tell that woman that I was going to write her son's obituary? I don't know why in the world you keep telling people that I am going to write their obituaries for them.

WEEDY: Can't nobody write them like you. Ev'rybody says that. Lettie Wentworth started tryin' to write them an' th' ones she wrote wasn't nothin'. Besides that, she can't read them like you can. Folks still talk about th' one you wrote an' recited for Emanuel Fisher. Reverend Goodlow told me he ain't never heard one like that in all his years of pastoring.

ALBERTA: Well, he's not going to hear it any more.

WEEDY: Brother, would you please tell me what's gotten into her?

DOC: Some sense.

WEEDY: [*Rises*] Well, give me that one you wrote for Emanuel Fisher. Maybe I can get somebody to change it around. . . .

ALBERTA: I threw it away.

WEEDY: You threw Emanuel Fisher's obituary away?

ALBERTA: Didn't I just say I did?

WEEDY: You mean you don't have a copy of it?

ALBERTA: What does "throw it away" mean?

WEEDY: Can't you remember the way it went and write it out?

ALBERTA: I have erased it from my mind.

WEEDY: Why?

ALBERTA: Because I didn't want to remember it.

WEEDY: An' I promised Reverend Goodlow I'd give him a copy of it. He wanted to make copies of it and send it around to his friends. You should have heard it, Brother. I tell you it was a movin' thing. . . . An' th' way Alberta read it . . . pure poetry.

DOC: Didn't have any figures in it, did it?

WEEDY: Ain't you got no respect for nothin' or

	nobody? [*To* ALBERTA] I bet if you put your mind to it . . . What did you call it?
ALBERTA:	The Flight of the Purple Angels.
WEEDY:	Tell Brother what it was about.
ALBERTA:	It was about . . . [*Comes into living room*] . . . the purple angels coming to take him home. Coming to take him to the land of glory . . .
WEEDY:	Alberta just got carried away, didn't you, Alberta?
ALBERTA:	Mama, you're going to be late for church.
DOC:	Yeah, you're holdin' me up.
WEEDY:	Brother ain't never heard it. Do it for Brother.
ALBERTA:	Mama, will you please go to church.
DOC:	[*Opens door*] Will you c'mon, Weedy, if you're goin'.
WEEDY:	[*Halfway out door*] If you're up when I get back I'll bring you some ice cream.
ALBERTA:	You don't have to bother.
WEEDY:	I thought you liked ice cream.
ALBERTA:	All right, Mama, bring me back some ice cream.
DOC:	[*Slightly off stage*] Weedy, are you comin' or not?
WEEDY:	Just a minute, please sir. Don't be so impatient. [*Kisses* ALBERTA *on forehead*] Now, be a good girl an' don't open th' door until you hear my voice. Lotta robbin' an' folks gettin' hit in th' head goin' on. Mother'll bring you some ice cream. [WEEDY *exits.*]

[ALBERTA *locks the door behind her. She goes into her bedroom and returns with a brown bag from which she removes several slips of paper. She is about to tear them up when the sound of the* CHOIR *is heard from the storefront church down the street.*]

THE STY OF THE BLIND PIG | 9

CHOIR: Near the Cross
Near the Cross
Keep my soul near the Cross . . .

[*The lights fade on* ALBERTA *holding the obituaries and listening to the* CHOIR.]

SCENE 2

The lights come up several days later in the afternoon. Beyond the window a heavy downpour of rain is heard along with the sound of thunder and the cracking of lightning. WEEDY *and* ALBERTA *are seated on the couch, both dressed in black, both in naked white light.*

WEEDY: Maybe we should have gone to the cemetery.

ALBERTA: [*Leaning back, trying to rest*] The cars were all filled up. Every funeral car was packed with his family.

WEEDY: We could have gone in one of the other cars. We could have squeezed in with Mother Hansen and her son.

ALBERTA: And haffta listen to that woman talk that crazy talk she talks. And her ole nutty son, Jimmy. I swear I don't believe he's got good sense.

WEEDY: Isaiah didn't have a load . . . we coulda rode with him.

ALBERTA: Mama, I asked him . . . said he'd be glad to drive us out but that we'd have to find another way back.

WEEDY: Coulda caught th' bus . . . ?

ALBERTA: You know how long it takes to get back from that cemetery by bus? We'd be all night getting back here.

WEEDY: Know Sister Martin'll think it's funny that I didn't go to the cemetery.

ALBERTA: I didn't see her trying to get us a ride. She didn't have our names on the list for the funeral cars.

WEEDY: Woman was upset. [*There is a pause.*]

THE STY OF THE BLIND PIG | 11

They really did a good job on him. Looked just like he looked in life. I remember when you and him use to be in the Sunshine Band.

ALBERTA: I don't remember him being in the Sunshine Band.

WEEDY: You don't remember being in the Sunshine Band with A. J. Martin?

ALBERTA: I don't remember ever seeing him before today.

WEEDY: Way y'all use to play around th' church when you were little.

ALBERTA: Funny I can't remember him . . . but he sure was a nice-looking man.

WEEDY: A. J. Martin was a fine-looking man.

ALBERTA: Who was that calling out for him? Kept screaming his name.

WEEDY: That was Lettie Wentworth. She was crazy about him. Hadn't been for Sister Martin I think A. J. might have married her. [*Slight pause*] She sure did perform this day. I mean she really put on a show.

ALBERTA: The way she was carrying on I thought he was going to raise up in that casket.

WEEDY: She sure did show out . . . just show out. [*Slight pause*] You sure did read that obituary. You had that whole church just stirred up. One woman just fell out and started kicking. Another one leaped up an' danced the dance of happiness.

ALBERTA: She sure scared me when she let out that scream.

WEEDY: You had her stirred up . . . full of the Holy Ghost. Wasn't one person in that church that wasn't touched by the Holy Ghost. All that hollerin' that Lettie Wentworth did didn't mean nothin'. And the way you read those telegrams . . . I tell you, Alberta, it was somethin' to behold. You have a gift . . . a callin'. Yes, Lord! [*Pause*] You almost scared me to death when you fell outta th' pulpit like that. You almost fell into th' casket. Fainted like that . . . sure scared me. [ALBERTA *moves to cupboard and pours herself a drink.*] You shouldn't be drinkin' that whiskey.

ALBERTA: I need something for my nerves.

WEEDY: That's what's givin' you them faintin' spells.

ALBERTA: I didn't have a fainting spell. . . . I just lost my balance, that's all.

WEEDY: The ushers had to come an' revive you.

ALBERTA: Mama, they just picked me up.

WEEDY: Keep on drinkin' that whiskey.

ALBERTA: I just lost my balance and fell. Maybe it was Lettie Wentworth doing all that screaming. . . . Got on my nerves.

WEEDY: Did you drink any of that whiskey before we went to the funeral?

ALBERTA: My nerves were bad.

WEEDY: You mean you were up in th' church . . . standin' in th' pulpit drunk as a skunk?

ALBERTA: I was not drunk. I just had a little taste.

WEEDY: No wonder you didn't want to go to the cemetery. Glad now we didn't go. Folks found out you were drunk . . . lawd, th' child, is just turnin' into a whiskey head. A whiskey head!

ALBERTA: I am not a whiskey head! And I wasn't drunk at the funeral.

WEEDY: Then why did you fall out for dead?

ALBERTA: I dunno. I just got weak all over . . . started having heat flashes . . .

WEEDY: Heat flashes?

ALBERTA: Shhhh!

WEEDY: Shhhh, what?

ALBERTA: Don't talk so loud.

WEEDY: Don't talk so loud?

ALBERTA: The walls have ears.

WEEDY: The walls have ears. Alberta, what's wrong with you? I don't know what in

THE STY OF THE BLIND PIG | 13

this world you're talkin' about. What'd you mean the walls have ears?

ALBERTA: It's just that someone may be listening to us.

WEEDY: Who's listening to us?

ALBERTA: [*Crosses to door*] Wait a minute . . . [*She places her ear to the door.*] Someone may be out there.

WEEDY: [*Moves to door*] Ain't nobody out there.

ALBERTA: How'd you know?

WEEDY: [*Opens door and looks out into hallway*] Ain't nobody out there. Ain't a soul out there.

ALBERTA: I thought I heard something.

WEEDY: [*Closes door and follows* ALBERTA *into living room*] Why don't you go lay down for a while?

ALBERTA: No, I don't want to lie down.

WEEDY: For a half hour or so.

ALBERTA: No! I don't want to lay down.

WEEDY: Don't carry on so.

ALBERTA: [*Moves to cupboard to refill her glass*] Just leave me alone, please.

WEEDY: You ain't gonna drink no more of that whiskey.

ALBERTA: Mama . . . please! . . . Jesus . . . please! Please! Please, Jesus!

WEEDY: You already not feelin' well.

ALBERTA: [*Crosses into her bedroom*] I'm all right. [*Slams door behind her*]

[WEEDY, *confused, moves to her rocking chair and looks out of window. She rocks denoting the passage of time.* ALBERTA *comes out of bedroom dressed in a maid's uniform.*]

WEEDY: Where you goin'?

ALBERTA: I promised Mrs. Coutrell that I'd serve a party for her if she let me off for the funeral. I bet she thinks I'm the biggest liar. . . . Everytime she looks around I'm taking time off for a funeral. I sure don't feel like going out there tonight.

WEEDY: Why don't you call her and tell her that you don't feel well?

ALBERTA: No, she'll be stuck. I told her that I would try my best to make it.

WEEDY: Let her serve her own party.

ALBERTA: [*Moves to door*] I'll see you later.

WEEDY: Alberta?

ALBERTA: Yes?

WEEDY: Never mind . . . nothin'.

[ALBERTA *exits as* WEEDY *rocks at window. The lights fade.*]

SCENE 3

The lights come up about a week later, at night. ALBERTA *is seated at the table making crepe-paper flowers. She works very intensely, completely involved in her task. Off stage we hear the sound of* BLIND JORDAN *singing and playing his guitar.*

BLIND JORDAN: Amazin' Grace how sweet it sounds
it saved a wretch like me
I once was lost but now I'm found
was blind but now I see. . . .

[*The voice stops in front of the door. We hear a soft tap.*]

ALBERTA: Who is it?
BLIND JORDAN: It's me, ma'm.
ALBERTA: Who?
BLIND JORDAN: Blind Jordan.
ALBERTA: Blind Jordan? Who do you want to see?
BLIND JORDAN: Grace Waters.
ALBERTA: Grace Waters? You must have the wrong apartment. There's no Grace Waters living here.
BLIND JORDAN: Can I speak to you for just one minute, ma'm?
ALBERTA: What for?
BLIND JORDAN: Please, ma'm . . . please.
ALBERTA: I told you no Grace Waters lives here.
BLIND JORDAN: Please . . . may I speak to you?
ALBERTA: Nobody by that name . . . [*She puts on the night latch and cracks the door open. Seeing that he is blind, she unlatches the door and opens it fully.*] Oh . . . come in . . . [*She leads him across threshold.*]

[*He is a tall, powerfully built man whose age is difficult to judge. He is dressed in a black shirt, with dark trousers and a black seaman's cap. A pair of dark glasses covers his eyes and across his shoulder he carries a battered guitar with a silver cup on the stock.*]

BLIND JORDAN: Thank you.

ALBERTA: [*Closing door*] Now, you say you're looking for a Grace Waters. Do you know which apartment she lives in?

BLIND JORDAN: No, ma'm, I sure don't. Ain't even sure she lives in this buildin'.

ALBERTA: Well, how . . . ?

BLIND JORDAN: I know she lives somewhere on State Street in Chicago. I just been goin' from buildin' to buildin' . . . door to door inquiring about her.

ALBERTA: Grace Waters . . . ? I don't know anybody, off hand, by that name in this building. She could be rooming. What does she look like? Oh, I'm sorry.

BLIND JORDAN: Ain't no need bein' sorry, ma'm. I'm use to it . . . been blind for a long time. That's part of my name . . . Blind Jordan. Don't reckon you've ever heard of me up here, but down home I'm known all th' way from East St. Louis to New Orleans. [*Pause*] Ma'm, I was wonderin' . . . would you be kind enough to give me a glass of water?

ALBERTA: Surely. [*Crosses to sink and gets glass of water, returns, places it in his hand*] Here you are.

BLIND JORDAN: [*Drinking*] Thank y', ma'm, thank y' kindly. [*Returns glass to her*] Just about to run dry. Can't seem to get use to this Chicago water. Takes a while, I reckon. [*Another pause*] You like music, ma'm?

ALBERTA: Yes, I like music.

BLIND JORDAN:	[*Takes guitar off shoulder*] Sure would like to play you a tune.
ALBERTA:	I'd like to hear you, but there's no one here but me.
BLIND JORDAN:	I don't mean you no harm, ma'm . . . no harm in this world.
ALBERTA:	[*Places glass in sink*] I'm not afraid, Mr. Jordan.
BLIND JORDAN:	Thought I might play a tune for y' in exchange for a little somethin' to eat.
ALBERTA:	Are you hungry, Mr. Jordan?
BLIND JORDAN:	Ma'm, I'm so hungry I'm weak.
ALBERTA:	[*She starts to help him, hesitates.*] C'mon into the kitchen.
BLIND JORDAN:	Could you direct me?
ALBERTA:	Certainly. [*Leads him to table*] Let me move some of this stuff out of your way. [*Places vase on sink*]
BLIND JORDAN:	[*Touching one of the paper flowers*] What's this?
ALBERTA:	Just something I made.
BLIND JORDAN:	Crepe-paper flower?
ALBERTA:	You know about crepe-paper flowers, Mr. Jordan?
BLIND JORDAN:	Yes'm. Made out of colored crepe-paper and paste . . . with pieces of wire for stems. Down home folks don't always have money for real flowers. So they make their own. I never like them . . . same with artificial fruit. . . . Oh, I'm sorry, ma'm. I didn't mean to belittle your gift.
ALBERTA:	I'd hardly call it a gift, Mr. Jordan. [*Opens ice box*] Now let me see what's in here.
BLIND JORDAN:	Oh, anything'll do me, ma'm. Don't haffta put yourself to no trouble whatsoever. Leftovers from your supper'll do me just fine.
ALBERTA:	[*Removes meat and bread*] I'll make you a sandwich . . . some milk.
BLIND JORDAN:	Thank you, ma'm. May I ask your name?
ALBERTA:	Alberta. Alberta Warren.

BLIND JORDAN: [*Singing*]
Alberta, let you hair hang low
Alberta, let your hair hang low
I'll give you more gold than your apron
can hold
If you just let your hair hang low

Alberta, what's on your mind
Alberta, what's on your mind
Because you keep me worried and
bothered all the time
Alberta, what's on your mind . . .

ALBERTA: [*Placing sandwich before him. Moving his
hands to sandwich and milk*] That was
very nice. I don't think I ever heard that
song before.

BLIND JORDAN: [*Eating*] My father taught me that song.
He was blind like me . . . runs in our
family. He was one of the great street
singers. Known all th' way from Vicksburg
to Jackson. Yes'm, they all knew Big Blind
Jordan . . . king of the twelve-string
guitar. [*Slight pause*] Usta be a lotta
blind street singers in them days, but now
ain't but a few of us left. They done all
passed away . . . faded in time with th'
comin' of the piccolo.

ALBERTA: How did you get here . . . to Chicago?

BLIND JORDAN: Part way by car . . . part way by foot.
Found th' direction an' just started puttin'
one foot in front of the other.

ALBERTA: How long have you been looking for her
. . . Grace Waters?

BLIND JORDAN: A long time. Sometimes it seems like I
ain't never not been lookin' for her.
[*Finishing his sandwich and milk*] Well,
I reckon I better be gettin' along.

ALBERTA: Let me get my coat and I'll help you
down the stairs.

BLIND JORDAN: No! No, thank y', ma'm. [*Rises from
table*] What's th' number of this buildin'?

THE STY OF THE BLIND PIG | 19

ALBERTA: Why it's era-era-era-era . . . [*Embarrassed*] It's the . . . I'm sorry. . . . Now, let me see? You want to know the number of this building? The number of this building is . . . 3868 State Street.

BLIND JORDAN: Thank you. I'll know where to start tomorrow.

ALBERTA: Do you have any money?

BLIND JORDAN: I'll walk and play until somebody puts something in my cup.

ALBERTA: [*Takes dollar from her purse*] Here. [*Puts dollar in his hand*]

BLIND JORDAN: Thank you, ma'm.

ALBERTA: [*Leads him to door*] And if you're ever hungry or tired . . .

BLIND JORDAN: Good night.

ALBERTA: [*Opens door and gently helps him out*] Good night. [*She closes door behind him.*]

BLIND JORDAN: [*Off stage, singing*]
Amazing Grace how sweet it sounds
It saved a wretch like me
I once was lost but now I'm found
Was blind but now I see . . .

[*The lights fade on* ALBERTA *standing watching the door.*]

SCENE 4

The lights fade in on a Saturday about a week later at midday. DOC *is seated at the table in the kitchen.* WEEDY *enters from* ALBERTA's *bedroom carrying a bottle of medicine. She places the bottle on the table next to several other bottles of medicine.*

WEEDY: Here's another one.

DOC: [*Looks off in another direction*] Unhuh.

WEEDY: [*Taking out her glasses*] This one ain't got the name of no doctor on it either. Now, why should she scratch the label off the bottle?

DOC: Maybe she figured you'd be ramblin' round in her room.

WEEDY: How could she think that? She ain't never caught me ramblin' round in her room. [*Examines bottles*] Pink pills? Lord, what in th' world is th' child doin' with all these pink pills?

DOC: If the voice of the Lord came outta that wall an' told you, I bet you'd break your neck gettin' outta here.

WEEDY: Brother, I want you to help me.

DOC: I ain't puttin' in no numbers for you. Haffta do that yourself.

WEEDY: I'll just wait until you get all through cuttin' th' fool.

DOC: [*Sighs*] All right, Weedy.

WEEDY: I want you to help me find out what doctor she's goin' to.

DOC: Why don't you just ask her?

WEEDY: If she intended to tell me don't you think she would have told me by now?

DOC: If she intended for you to know I reckon she would have.

WEEDY: She goes to the doctor on Saturday . . . bound she's there now. Now next Saturday you could be parked outside . . . follow her . . .

DOC: Spy on her?

WEEDY: I ain't askin' you to spy on her. All I'm askin' you to do is to find out what doctor she's goin' to.

DOC: Just how much are you plannin' to pay me for this service?

WEEDY: Pay you?

DOC: As long as I'm goin' into undercover work —which I am told is very dangerous—I feel like I should get paid. Espionage is a very expensive proposition.

WEEDY: You wanna get paid to aid your own flesh and blood?

DOC: Aid? I should've given aid a long time ago. [*Rises, moves to cupboard*] But to that girl . . . not to you. [*Pours himself a drink*] Only she ain't a girl no more. She's gettin' to be . . . You got salvation, but what she got?

WEEDY: I ain't interested in all that ole random talk. All I'm interested in is whether or not you're gonna help me.

DOC: Salvation? What is it exactly you saved folks're saved from?

WEEDY: From plagues like you.

DOC: Y'know, Weedy, for fifteen cents I'd cut off a mop handle, make a short stick and get somethin' done.

WEEDY: Are you goin' to help me find out who her doctor is?

DOC: Ain't nothin' wrong with Alberta.

WEEDY: Oh, you've commence to practice medicine.

DOC: Y'know . . . she's beginnin' to look like you.

WEEDY: Who she suppose to look like?

DOC: Not like you.

WEEDY: Well, y'know you ain't no springtime beauty.

DOC: That ain't what them little, pretty young girls tell me.

WEEDY: They oughta tell you what a big fool you are. What young girl would want your ole gray, rusty behind. Everytime you walk across th' floor your bones done commence to creak.

DOC: Pearl likes it.

WEEDY: Just shows she ain't got good sense. And don't you bring that thing in my house no more. Both of y'all ridin' down State Street on a bicycle . . . her with her dress tucked in her bloomers . . . an' th' both of you drunk. I just held my head in shame when I saw you two fools comin'.

DOC: She sure do look like Nora Lee . . . spittin' image of her.

WEEDY: Woman don't look like Nora Lee . . . nothin' like her.

DOC: You just don't like her.

WEEDY: I ain't got no thoughts about her. Except she's a nut.

DOC: At least she ain't always sick.

WEEDY: Nora Lee couldn't help it 'cause she was frail.

DOC: Is that why you liked Nora Lee? You upheld her in her misery. Now you got Alberta pullin' th' same trick.

WEEDY: I got her . . . [*Mimicking herself*] Oh, now, I done told her, Alberta, you run around and play like you're sick.

DOC: Didn't haffta tell her. Way you moaned an' groaned . . . talkin' all th' time about somethin' bein' wrong with you.

WEEDY: Keep on, you gonna be done made me tell you somethin'.

DOC: Tell me what?

THE STY OF THE BLIND PIG | 23

WEEDY: To kiss my foot.

DOC: Better be careful, girl. You'll be swearin' directly.

WEEDY: You're enough to make the angels in heaven swear.

DOC: Why don't you have a little drink?

WEEDY: You better get away from around me.

DOC: [*Comes to her*] Hey, how about a little sugar?

WEEDY: Will you not be slobberin' all over me, please sir, with that whiskey smell.

DOC: The smell of a happy soul.

[*The door opens and* ALBERTA *enters. There has been a change in her appearance. She wears a tailored suit and hat. Her hair has been combed out and styled.*]

ALBERTA: Hello, Mama . . . Uncle Doc. [*Sees medicine on table*] How did my medicine get out here?

WEEDY: I was just showin' Brother how appetizin' they're makin' medicine nowadays. Wasn't I, Brother?

ALBERTA: [*Looks at* DOC, *who looks away*] I wish you wouldn't ramble through my room. [*Gathers up bottles*] Stop spying on me.

WEEDY: Ain't nobody spyin' on you, crazy woman. Who'd you think is interested in your medicine? [*Hollering out to* ALBERTA, *who has entered her room with the bottles*] An' you needn' be scratchin' the labels offa the bottles to keep me from knowin' who your doctor is.

ALBERTA: [*At door*] Oh, that's why you were rambling through my things? [*Looks at* DOC] You in on this too?

DOC: I was just bein' recruited for the secret service. Detailed to trail you . . .

WEEDY: Well sir, I wasn't sure before you didn't have good sense, but now there is no

	doubt in my mind whatsoever.
ALBERTA:	Will you please not ask people to spy on me?
WEEDY:	I ain't askin' nobody to spy on you.
DOC:	Didn't you ask me to find out who her doctor was?
WEEDY:	Will you shut up? Have you taken complete loss of your mind? Won't be long before the men in the white coats'll be on your tail . . . carryin' you out there to Kankakee insane asylum. I believe you done lost your mind. Got no business runnin' round loose.
DOC:	How you gonna stay saved bearin' false witness?
ALBERTA:	Why don't you call in the police . . . send a letter to Mr. Hoover? You better stop it, Mama. You just better stop. One day, I swear to God, I'll walk out of here and never look back.
WEEDY:	Will you, please, not take the Lord's name in vain in my presence? Sound like some old street woman.
ALBERTA:	You have tried my patience for thirty-odd years. Eating up the food I buy. Sleeping out the bed clothes I have to buy. And on top of that drivin' me out of what little mind I have left! I'm so tired of it, sometimes I just wanna run down the street and scream.
WEEDY:	Well, now, you just let me straighten out your behind before you go too far. I don't have to stay here an' take this kind of abuse. Before I'll take abuse from a child I birth into the world, I will pick manure with the birds. [*She crosses into bedroom.*] Don't haffta stay here an' take this kinda talk.

[*After a moment* ALBERTA *moves to the bedroom and stands at door.*]

THE STY OF THE BLIND PIG | 25

DOC:	What she doin'?
ALBERTA:	Packing.
DOC:	Is she movin' out again?
ALBERTA:	Unhuh.
WEEDY:	[*Enters*] Got too much grit in my craw to stay any place I ain't wanted. [*She is carrying a small suitcase.*]
ALBERTA:	Where're you going this time?
WEEDY:	Anywhere away from here. Before I'll stay where I ain't wanted I'll take up residence in the old folks' home.
DOC:	Weedy, you'd worry those folks to death.
WEEDY:	Just because I'm concerned with your health that's no reason for you to mistreat me. I never said a harsh word to my mother the longest day she walked this earth. Spyin' on you. You have not heard me say one single, solitary thing about spyin' on you. Have you heard me utter one halfa syllable about spyin' on you? But if you want to listen to the random talk of folks, who are fugitives from the authorities at the Kankakee insane asylum, you go right ahead. [*She has moved into kitchen.*] And you needn't worry about me . . . 'cause I got grit in my craw . . . always did have. I give you up in the hands of the Lord, 'cause I have fought the good fight. [*She moves into the hall near the door.*] If you wanna go sneakin' off to a doctor and not tell nobody about the nature of your complaint, nothin' I can do. [*Opens door*] If you don't tell me, your own mother, who underwent the pains of death to bring you into this world, who struggled with you after your father ran off and left you without a crust of bread on which to exercise your stomach muscles, who worked like the very dog to put shoes on your feet an' give you a place to lay your head. Lord,

that's why I got this hurtin' in my side now . . . done almost work myself to death supportin' folks. [*She pauses.*] When I close my eyes in death you're gonna realize that I was the best friend you ever had.

ALBERTA: Goodbye, Mama.

WEEDY: All right. [*Exits*]

DOC: Where'd you think she'll go?

ALBERTA: Around the corner to have some ice cream with some chocolate syrup on it.

DOC: [*Crosses to window*] Know what you oughta do? Run like hell! Run like the building was on fire. Run for parts unknown. Satchel up and go if you gotta leave here walking.

ALBERTA: Run? Run where?

DOC: What about Mrs. Coutrell? Ain't she been after you to stay on th' place?

ALBERTA: Yes.

DOC: Get a day off . . . come see Weedy.

ALBERTA: Mrs. Coutrell is almost as bad as Mama. She works my tongue pallet out now. I know what she would do if I was livin' there. She'd be havin' parties ev'rynight . . . to show her friends that she had a gal stayin' on th' place. [*Pause*] I hear her on the phone now talking about me. Promising people to loan me out to them . . . like I was some kind of thing. [*Pause*] I don't know what she and Mr. Coutrell think I am. Telling me I'm a member of the family. Just like one of the family. What I oughta do . . . is one night after I fix dinner . . . is to sit down with them at the table. See if they'll let one of the family sit down and eat with them. [*Pause*] Accusing me of stealing their whiskey?

DOC: I thought they gave it to you.

THE STY OF THE BLIND PIG | 27

ALBERTA: No, I steal it. And everything else I can get my hands on that they got.

DOC: Keep on, they're gonna have your behind arrested.

ALBERTA: Mr. Coutrell would never stand for that. He wouldn't have my behind to pinch any more.

DOC: He does that?

ALBERTA: He's been pinching my behind since the first day I walked into that house, fifteen years ago.

DOC: [*Gets himself another drink*] Sure wish that I could . . . [*Slight pause*] In the old days down on Beale Street . . . I usta handle a lotta money. Lotta money! Wouldn't been nothin' for me to walk up an' hand you a couple of hundred. Always had that kinda money in my pocket! [*Reflects*] Your ole uncle . . . was a legend on that street. Carried a diamond stick pin an' a pistol in my pocket at all times. Nobody woulda dare mess with none of my kinfolks. Don't care who he was. Cause Sportin' Jimmy Sweet didn't take no mess!

ALBERTA: I can handle Mr. Coutrell.

DOC: You oughta quit . . . find yourself another job. Why don't you quit?

ALBERTA: One place is like another.

DOC: You wouldn't have to take no mess like that. [*Slight pause*] Is it them brats?

ALBERTA: Janet and Johnny? They're almost grown now. Two or three years and they'll be going off to college. Maybe I'll leave then.

DOC: Why wait for them to leave?

ALBERTA: I promised them . . .

DOC: Promised them what?

ALBERTA: That I wouldn't go away until they got grown. They probably don't even remember that now.

DOC: When did you promise them that?

ALBERTA: When they were little. They use to leave them alone so much.

DOC: You got too involved with those chaps. They'll go on about their business. In a few years th' only thing they'll remember about you is your name. And they'll have to think about that.

ALBERTA: They're forgetting me now. I see. They don't seem to remember things we use to do when they were little. Places I use to take them . . .

DOC: I remember once you brought them around to the shine parlor where I worked. Now, ain't that somethin'? Sportin' Jimmy Sweet—a shoeshine boy!

[*There is a knock on door.*]

ALBERTA: There's Mama now. [*Gets up from couch and moves to door*] Must've forgotten her key. [*Opens door, admits* BLIND JORDAN] Oh, hi, c'mon in. My uncle is here. [*She assists him into living room to meet* DOC.] Mr. Sweet, this is Mr. Jordan.

BLIND JORDAN: [*Extending his hand*] Please to make your acquaintance, Mr. Sweet.

DOC: [*Shaking his hand*] How'd y' do?

BLIND JORDAN: You haven't by any chance heard of a woman named Grace Waters, have you, Mr. Sweet?

DOC: Grace Waters?

ALBERTA: Jordan is looking for her. Came all the way up from the old country searching for her.

DOC: Where about in th' big foot country are you from?

BLIND JORDAN: Sort of all over.

DOC: [*Slight pause*] Grace Waters. Naw, don't recollect meetin' anybody by that name. Chicago's a big place to be lookin' for

	somebody unless y' know where to put your hand on them.
BLIND JORDAN:	I'll find her.
DOC:	Well, I reckon I'd better be pickin' up Pearl. Told her I'd pick her up after work. [*He moves toward door.*] Oh, by th' way . . . ain't had no good dreams lately, have y'?
BLIND JORDAN:	You play th' numbers, Mr. Sweet?
DOC:	Been known to drop a dollar on a figure once in a while.
BLIND JORDAN:	Try triple zeros.
DOC:	[*Writes it down*] Triple zero? Sounds good. 'Course, they all sound good.
BLIND JORDAN:	Get on it . . . stay on it. It's gonna fall soon.
DOC:	How soon?
BLIND JORDAN:	Well, I can't give you the exact date . . . but it won't be long.
DOC:	All right, I'll get on it for a while. See you, Alberta, Mr. Jordan. [*He exits.*]
BLIND JORDAN:	Good night, Mr. Sweet.

[ALBERTA *closes door behind* DOC, *then comes back into living room.*]

ALBERTA:	I didn't know you'd be around this evening.
BLIND JORDAN:	Thought I'd try to get through that big buildin' this evenin' . . . th' one we stopped at th' other day.
ALBERTA:	That's an awfully big building, Jordan. Might take two or three days to get through it.
BLIND JORDAN:	All I got is time.
ALBERTA:	And it's Saturday . . . getting late. Folks don't like to be disturbed on Saturday evening.
BLIND JORDAN:	They don't have to open the door. All they got to do is to say whether or not Grace Waters is livin' there.

ALBERTA:	Suppose she was living in that big building. Suppose we knocked on the right door. All she would have to do is to say that she didn't live there and we'd walk right on away.
BLIND JORDAN:	I know her voice too well for that.
ALBERTA:	Somebody else could answer the door and say she didn't live there.
BLIND JORDAN:	If I come within a hundred feet of her I'll know it.
ALBERTA:	You know how many buildings there are in this neighborhood? You know how long it'll take you to knock on every door around here?
BLIND JORDAN:	I'll get around to all of 'em. I don't care how long it takes.
ALBERTA:	Half the buildings around here are under the order of condemnation.
BLIND JORDAN:	That's why I need you to help me. Point out the ones that still got people livin' in them.
ALBERTA:	It's not that I don't want to help you, Jordan . . .
BLIND JORDAN:	The other evenin' when you went around with me . . . saved me a lot of time.
ALBERTA:	You can't find anyone going from door to door. . . . Wandering through these ole, deserted buildings you could fall and hurt yourself.
BLIND JORDAN:	That's why I need your eyes.
ALBERTA:	Someone . . . some of these kids could attack us . . . try to rob us. There was a pair around here not too long ago—they called them tall and short man—was robbing people in their own hallways.
BLIND JORDAN:	Are you afraid?
ALBERTA:	No, I'm not afraid.
BLIND JORDAN:	You think I can't protect you. Think because of my affliction you ain't safe with me.
ALBERTA:	What could you do with two men?

THE STY OF THE BLIND PIG | 31

BLIND JORDAN:	You don't have to worry none with me.
ALBERTA:	Suppose they had a gun? Tall and short man use to hold people up at gun point. That's why so many people won't open their doors.
BLIND JORDAN:	Tall and short man with or without a gun don't worry me none.
ALBERTA:	Jordan, what could you do against two men with a gun?
BLIND JORDAN:	You're saying that you don't want to help me.
ALBERTA:	Maybe it's just that I'm tired.
BLIND JORDAN:	I reckon it is an exhaustin' thing . . . help me.
ALBERTA:	Why don't we wait and do it tomorrow? Tomorrow is Sunday. Tomorrow afternoon would be a good day. About the time people get home from church. People are in a better mood then.
BLIND JORDAN:	I had my mind set on this evening.
ALBERTA:	Why can't you wait until tomorrow?
BLIND JORDAN:	Lose a whole day.
ALBERTA:	You said you had all the time in the world to look for her.
BLIND JORDAN:	I don't want to lose a whole day.
ALBERTA:	All right then, go on! But you can go by yourself. Now, I'm perfectly willing to help you if you wait until tomorrow. Since you can't wait—go right ahead. And I hope you fall and break your neck!
BLIND JORDAN:	What?
ALBERTA:	I'm sorry, I didn't mean that, Jordan.
BLIND JORDAN:	You're upset? Have I done somethin' to you?
ALBERTA:	No.
BLIND JORDAN:	Then what is it?
ALBERTA:	It's got nothing to do with you.
BLIND JORDAN:	You want to tell me?
ALBERTA:	There's nothing to tell.
BLIND JORDAN:	[*After a pause*] I reckon I should be getting along.

ALBERTA: Maybe so.

WEEDY: [*Enters*] Aw, I didn't know you had company.

ALBERTA: [*As* WEEDY *comes into living room*] Oh, Mama? Mama, this is Mr. Jordan. Jordan this is my mother, Mrs. Wenella Warren.

BLIND JORDAN: Mrs. Warren.

WEEDY: How do you do.

ALBERTA: I didn't expect you back so soon.

WEEDY: I only came back for a minute. While waitin' for th' bus I had an acute attack of th' miss-meal cramp. You ever had an acute attack of th' miss-meal cramp, Mr. Jordan, sir?

BLIND JORDAN: I've had so many wrinkles in my stomach sometimes it's felt like a prune.

WEEDY: Well, you must stay for supper.

BLIND JORDAN: Wouldn't want to put you out none.

WEEDY: [*Takes him by arm and leads him into kitchen*] You ain't puttin' us out none. Alberta likes company. [*Seats him at table and sits down herself*] Don't you, Alberta?

ALBERTA: [*At refrigerator*] How do you think some warmed-up pork chops would be?

WEEDY: In this warm weather? My stomach wouldn't have time to settle before my bedtime. And I sure ain't goin' to go to bed with no pork unsettled in my stomach to die durin' th' night from an attack of the acute indigestion. Mr. Jordan, sir, did you ever know anybody to die from an attack of th' acute indigestion, brought on by th' eatin' of pork in warm weather?

BLIND JORDAN: Yes'm . . . I knew a man down home once who had a naggin' wife. Lived about twenty-five miles below New Orleans. Well, sir, one night in August he fixed that woman some pork chops. She died that very same night from an attack of

THE STY OF THE BLIND PIG | 33

	the acute indigestion. Of course, later on they found out he fried them in lye.
WEEDY:	[*Uncomfortable*] You know some strange folks.
ALBERTA:	Mama, he's joking.
WEEDY:	Are you jokin' with me, Mr. Jordan, sir?
ALBERTA:	Tell her you're joking. Otherwise she'll swear I'm trying to poison her.
BLIND JORDAN:	I'm kidding you, Mrs. Warren.
WEEDY:	Oh, you're a kidder, Mr. Jordan. Always liked a kidder. Yes sir, the one thing I always did like was a kidder. How long you been a kidder, Mr. Jordan, sir? Remember a man down in my home who was a kidder. "Kidding Sidney" they use to call him. Always like to kid folks. One day Kidding Sidney kidded the wrong man . . . an' he shot poor Kidding Sidney right dead in his mouth. An' Kidding Sidney didn't kid no more.
ALBERTA:	[*After a pause*] I'll make some hamburger.
WEEDY:	Are you an eater of hamburger, Mr. Kidder? Excuse me, I mean Mr. Jordan.
BLIND JORDAN:	I'm not a choosy eater.
WEEDY:	Never will I eat the flesh of a horse.
BLIND JORDAN:	Hamburger is from a cow.
WEEDY:	How do you know? Were you there when they slaughtered th' animal?
ALBERTA:	Suppose I just make some pork 'n' beans?
WEEDY:	That's what they feed convicts.
BLIND JORDAN:	You don't have to fix me nothin', Alberta.
WEEDY:	Ain't you gonna eat, Mr. Jordan?
BLIND JORDAN:	No, ma'm . . . I reckon I done lost my appetite. [*Rises from table*] Reckon I'll be gettin' along, Alberta.
ALBERTA:	All right, I'll see you to the door. [*She leads him through the living room to door.*]
BLIND JORDAN:	Good night, Mrs. Warren. Thank y' kindly for your hospitality.

WEEDY: Good night, Mr. Kidder . . . I mean Mr.
           Jordan.
ALBERTA: [*Closes door behind* JORDAN *and comes
           back into kitchen*] I wish you'd learn how
           to act nice.
WEEDY: I don't haffta learn how to act nice. I
           ain't runnin' for office. I've been elected.
           [*She rises from table and moves to her
           rocking chair.*]
ALBERTA: I thought you were hungry.
WEEDY: Done lost my appetite too, I reckon.
           [*Peers out of window*] Well, sir, they're
           still up there. Alberta!
ALBERTA: [*Running into living room*] What's the
           matter?
WEEDY: Come here quick.
ALBERTA: [*Moves to window*] What is it?
WEEDY: Corner building . . . three windows up.
           Look at those curtains.
ALBERTA: What about them?
WEEDY: I'm gonna write that woman a letter to-
           morrow. Dear Miss, whatever you name
           is, if you would just put a little bleach in
           your water you could get those dingy cur-
           tains you got hanging up there white. Slip
           down there and put it in her mailbox.
ALBERTA: Be sure to sign it so they can commit you
           to Kankakee. [*She crosses into her bed-
           room and returns with a sweater thrown
           around her shoulders.*]
WEEDY: Where you goin'?
ALBERTA: Catch some air.
WEEDY: With th' blind man?
ALBERTA: His name is Jordan, Mama.
WEEDY: I didn't mean no harm.
ALBERTA: Maybe I'll take a walk with him.
WEEDY: Sure hate to be here all by myself. Sup-
           pose I had a stroke while you were
           galavantin' up an' down th' street?
ALBERTA: [*Standing in the open door*] You're not
           going to have a stroke.

THE STY OF THE BLIND PIG | 35

WEEDY:	Howd'you know? Is the Almighty consultin' you 'bout his plans? Could lay right up here with my mouth all twisted up like poor Molly Ross.
ALBERTA:	Molly Ross?
BLIND JORDAN:	[*From the street below*] Thro' man-y dangers, toils and snares I have already come . . .
ALBERTA:	That's Jordan singing.
WEEDY:	Lived down the block . . . across th' street.
BLIND JORDAN:	'Tis Grace hath bro't me safe thus far And Grace will lead me home . . .
ALBERTA:	Molly Ross?
WEEDY:	Died today, poor woman.
BLIND JORDAN:	When we've been there ten thousand years Bright shining as the sun . . .
ALBERTA:	I don't think I knew her.
WEEDY:	'Course you didn't! You never paid her no attention. She wasn't none of your equal.
ALBERTA:	What did she look like?
BLIND JORDAN:	I've so few days to sing her praise Than when I first begun . . .
WEEDY:	Stout woman walked with a cane. Lawd, she sure was fat. Never seen a woman her age that fat before.
ALBERTA:	Oh, that woman . . . what was her name? Molly Ross?
BLIND JORDAN:	Amazing Grace how sweet the sound That saved a wretch like me . . .
WEEDY:	She sure was a good company keeper. Use to keep me company all day long.
ALBERTA:	Mama!
WEEDY:	Yes, sir, she sure was a good company keeper.
BLIND JORDAN:	I once was lost but now am found Was blind but now I see . . .

[*The lights fade.*]

ACT II ● ● ●

SCENE 1

The lights fade in on WEEDY *and* ALBERTA
*about two weeks later. It is now the first
Saturday in September and the sunlight
which fills the apartment has a touch of
gray in it.* WEEDY, *dressed in a stiff white
uniform, is packing a second white uniform into an open suitcase along with
several small articles. Throughout her
packing she moves to the window and
looks out onto the street several times.*
ALBERTA *is in the kitchen ironing a third
white uniform, alternating that task with
the making of sandwiches, which she
places in a shoe box on the table.*

WEEDY: [*Hollering to* ALBERTA *in kitchen*] I
wonder if I should take a coat?

ALBERTA: [*Bringing white dress and sandwiches
into living room. She begins to stuff them
into the suitcase.*] Maybe you oughta take
one just in case it turns cold.

WEEDY: Generally, shirt-sleeve weather down
there.

ALBERTA: [*Having difficulty packing suitcase*] This
suitcase ain't big enough. You shoulda
took mine.

WEEDY: Yours is too big and clumsy.

ALBERTA: You got too much stuff in here.

THE STY OF THE BLIND PIG | 37

WEEDY:	Same amount I always put in there ev'ry year.
ALBERTA:	Maybe the suitcase has gotten smaller. Let me get mine.
WEEDY:	Ain't nothin' wrong with that suitcase— not a thing.
ALBERTA:	[*Trying to lock it*] Well, I can't get it closed.
WEEDY:	Let me try. [*Struggling with it*]
ALBERTA:	[*Has gone into* WEEDY's *room and returns with a spring coat*] Get it closed?
WEEDY:	Naw. Maybe you better try again.
ALBERTA:	[*Putting spring coat in suitcase*] Never get it closed now. [WEEDY *tries again as* ALBERTA *goes into her room and comes back with a larger suitcase.*] Mama, why don't we just take everything out and pack it in here?
WEEDY:	[*Struggling to close the suitcase*] I don't want that thing. Don't want to be bothered with it.
ALBERTA:	Why? Bigger . . . and almost brand new.
WEEDY:	I like this one.
ALBERTA:	Mama, you can't get this thing closed.
WEEDY:	[*Takes coat out*] Here. [*Sits on it*] Fasten it quick!
ALBERTA:	[*Trying to snap the locks*] This thing is gonna bust wide open.
WEEDY:	Ain't never bust on me before.
ALBERTA:	[*Still trying to lock it*] You must have more in there this time.
WEEDY:	You just lock it.
ALBERTA:	[*Getting it locked*] Hope it don't jump open on you on the train. All your underwear in the aisle.
WEEDY:	Well, if folks ain't never seen underwear before, they won't know what it is.
ALBERTA:	What you gonna do about this coat?
WEEDY:	I don't reckon I really need it.
ALBERTA:	Could carry it over your arm.
WEEDY:	I don't feel like foolin' with it.

ALBERTA: Suit yourself. But suppose it turns cold?

WEEDY: It ain't gonna turn cold. [*There is a pause.*] Sure do wish you were comin' with me. You ain't never been to th' convocation. Oughta go once in your life.

ALBERTA: I can't afford to go!

WEEDY: I'd help you on your ticket.

ALBERTA: I can't get off my job for two weeks.

WEEDY: Why don't you just call up Mrs. Coutrell and tell her that you have to go out of town for two weeks, take care of some business?

ALBERTA: I can't afford to lose the money. Besides, I don't want to go down to Montgomery fooling with them crackers.

WEEDY: You don't have to fool with no crackers.

ALBERTA: Here tell they got laughing barrels all over the street down in Montgomery. Negro sees something funny he has to stick his head in the barrel and laugh.

WEEDY: Now, who told you that lie?

ALBERTA: I heard about it.

WEEDY: [*After a pause*] We sure would have a good time down there at the convocation. You'd get a chance to hear some of the best preaching you ever heard in your life. Best preachers in the country—from all over these United States—gather down there for th' convocation. An' I don't mean them what's learn it in th' school house. I'm talkin' 'bout them that's got th' callin'. Them that had to go off somewhere an' learn it are so dull an' dry. Near 'bouts puts me to sleep. But them that's got th' callin'—they can stir you up! Yes, Jesus, they can get you so worked up you'll think you're sittin' on your throne in glory. An' th' song battles. You ain't never in your born days heard no singin' like you hear at th' convocation. I tell you, Alberta, it is an inspirin' thing th' way some of them folks sing. I mean they can really sing! It's like Jesus had put th' voices in their mouths. And there's plenty for young folks to do too. Goin' 'round to th' different church socials. An' if th' weather is nice, they have a big outdoor picnic almost everyday. Then that evenin' the B.Y.P.U. —Baptist Young People's Union—have their little things in th' basement of th' church. 'Course, now, I don't have no truck with them Baptist folks, but you could go. [*Pause*] Sure see a lotta folks down there at th' convocation. A whole lotta folks you be done half forgotten— done slipped right outta your mind. Woman came up to me at th' last convocation and said to me, "Ain't you Wenella Sweet?" Lawd, I looked at that woman an' didn't know who in th' world she was. I couldn't place her to save my life. An' y' know she wouldn't tell me who she was. She just walked on away. [*Another slight pause*] I was on th' train on my way back to Chicago before it came to me who that woman was. Her name was Flora Jackson. She use to live right next door to me in Clarksdale, Mississippi. I knew her before you were born. Before I was even thinkin' about gettin' married. We went to school together. She sure didn't look like herself. Never would have known her in a million years if she hadn't recognized me. Flora Jackson! Prettiest girl you ever did see . . .

ALBERTA: How long had it been since you'd seen her?

WEEDY: Lawd, I don't reckon I had seen that woman in somethin' like fifty years. She had completely passed out of my mind. You oughta come with me, Alberta . . .

ALBERTA:	Mama, I don't want to go to the convocation. We can't even afford for you to go.
WEEDY:	Convocation is about the only little pleasure I get out of life. That and church.
ALBERTA:	Money you're going down there and throwing away—we could use that money to fix up this apartment.
WEEDY:	What's wrong with this apartment?
ALBERTA:	The furniture is old—worn out. I'd like to get some new pieces for the living room.
WEEDY:	Ain't nothin' wrong with this furniture.
ALBERTA:	It's older than the hills.
WEEDY:	Whole lot better than the junk they are makin' today.
ALBERTA:	At least I could get some slip covers to put over it. That big chair needs to be reupholstered. And the couch! That thing should have been thrown out years ago.
WEEDY:	That couch is still good.
ALBERTA:	While you're gone I think I'll have somebody come up and take that thing outta here.
WEEDY:	And what we gonna do for a couch?
ALBERTA:	I'll try to get a new one.
WEEDY:	Now, you leave that couch right alone. Had that couch before you were born.
ALBERTA:	The springs are comin' through. Everytime I sit on it it sticks right in my behind.
WEEDY:	Then keep your behind off of it.
ALBERTA:	Mrs. Coutrell got a couch stored in her garage. Maybe I could buy it from her. It ain't that good, but it's sure better than that one.
WEEDY:	Don't let me come back here and find that couch missing!
ALBERTA:	Well, I'm sure gonna get rid of it.
WEEDY:	No, you ain't! What's gotten into you? Gonna just throw my things out without my permission.

THE STY OF THE BLIND PIG | 41

ALBERTA:	You love that damned, wore-out ole couch so much, why don't you stay here and watch it?
WEEDY:	Now, how am I gonna stay here and watch it if I'm goin' to th' convocation? Talk silly.
ALBERTA:	Don't go! Stay here and watch it. Nail it down before you leave.
WEEDY:	I don't haffta nail it down. It's mine. You ain't got no business foolin' with it.
ALBERTA:	[*Goes into kitchen and gets hammer and nails*] I'll nail it down for you.
WEEDY:	What you fixin' to do?
ALBERTA:	[*Bends down to foot of couch*] I'm gonna nail it down.
WEEDY:	Don't you be puttin' no nails in my furniture.
ALBERTA:	I wanna make sure it's here when you come back.
WEEDY:	Give me that hammer.
ALBERTA:	No, I'm gonna make sure that nobody can move this piece of junk outta here.
WEEDY:	Now, you can put a nail in my furniture if you want to.
ALBERTA:	I'm gonna nail every piece of furniture in this house down. Make sure that when you come back it's just like you left it.
WEEDY:	[*Snatches hammer from her*] You better get somewhere an' sit down.
ALBERTA:	Then you nail it down.
WEEDY:	Just don't let me come back and find nothin' missin' outta here. 'Cause if I do . . .
ALBERTA:	What?
WEEDY:	You just take anythin' outta here an' you'll see what. Fool around directly and make me mad. [*Moves to kitchen and puts hammer away. Hears* ALBERTA *mumbling to herself.*] What's that you're sayin'?
ALBERTA:	Nothing.
WEEDY:	Well, don't be makin' all them ole funny

	sounds. 'Cause I think you're talkin' about me.
ALBERTA:	I'm talking to myself. Not thinking about you.
WEEDY:	Let me know it then. [*There is a pause.* WEEDY *has come back into the living room. She moves to the couch and places the suitcase on the floor.*] Lawd, have mercy.
ALBERTA:	What?
WEEDY:	I forgot to put on my white stockin's.
ALBERTA:	Where are they?
WEEDY:	In the suitcase. Think I should open it again? Might not get it closed before Brother gets here.
ALBERTA:	I guess I could go out to Thirty-ninth Street and get you another pair.
WEEDY:	Would you do that for Mother?
ALBERTA:	All right. [*Gets her bag and moves to door*] I'll run down there and get 'em.
WEEDY:	Hurry back before Brother gets here.
ALBERTA:	[*Opens door*] I'll get back as quick as I can. [*She exits.*]

[WEEDY *has moved to her rocking chair at the window and begins to rock. The lights dim to denote the passing of a few minutes.* BLIND JORDAN *appears in the door that* ALBERTA *has left open.* WEEDY *senses his presence and turns around to see him.*]

WEEDY:	Oh, it's you, Mr. Jordan. C'mon in.
BLIND JORDAN:	Alberta here?
WEEDY:	She just stepped out for a minute. You can c'mon in an' sit down.
BLIND JORDAN:	[*Making his way to big chair*] Thank y', ma'm.
WEEDY:	Seem to make your way around in this apartment pretty good.
BLIND JORDAN:	Don't take me too long to get use to a place.

THE STY OF THE BLIND PIG | 43

WEEDY:	I can see that stickin' out.
BLIND JORDAN:	Ma'm?
WEEDY:	[*Slight pause*] You and Alberta done got right friendly.
BLIND JORDAN:	Yes'm.
WEEDY:	Know I'm goin' to th' convocation?
BLIND JORDAN:	You goin' away?
WEEDY:	Catchin' th' train tonight for th' convocation. Be gone for two weeks.
BLIND JORDAN:	Alberta goin' with you?
WEEDY:	No, she's not goin'. [*Slight pause*] I was wonderin', Mr. Jordan, if you'd do me a favor?
BLIND JORDAN:	Anythin' I can, Mrs. Warren.
WEEDY:	Would you mind not comin' around here while I'm away?
BLIND JORDAN:	You mind if I ask why?
WEEDY:	You know why, Mr. Jordan.
BLIND JORDAN:	I do.
WEEDY:	I know you. You're the devil, Mr. Jordan. An' my daughter done open th' door for you and beckoned you to come in.
BLIND JORDAN:	You don't really believe I'm th' devil, Mrs. Warren.
WEEDY:	I didn't just come into th' world yesterday, y'know. I know you . . . know who you are.
BLIND JORDAN:	Who do you think I am?
WEEDY:	I been seein' all you old blind street singers all the days of my life. I know where you been and what you done done. I even know how you got blind, Mr. Jordan.
BLIND JORDAN:	I was born blind.
WEEDY:	I know that.
BLIND JORDAN:	You do?
WEEDY:	Probably come from a long line of blind street singers.
BLIND JORDAN:	Yes'm, I do. How did you know that? Alberta tell you?
WEEDY:	My eye commence to jump th' minute I saw you. An' when my eye commences

	to jump somethin' ain't right. There's danger afoot.
BLIND JORDAN:	Yes'm.
WEEDY:	An' this woman you're lookin' for?
BLIND JORDAN:	Grace Waters.
WEEDY:	You're still lookin' for her?
BLIND JORDAN:	I dunno. Lately I ain't sure that I am. All I know is that now when I knock on doors I sorta hope that she won't be there. That thought has crossed my mind several times lately.
WEEDY:	You keep on lookin' for her, Mr. Jordan.
BLIND JORDAN:	Why?
WEEDY:	You know why.
BLIND JORDAN:	Alberta?
WEEDY:	That's right, Mr. Jordan. You know exactly what I'm talkin' about.
BLIND JORDAN:	Ma'm . . . Alberta is . . .
WEEDY:	Not for you. No way whatsoever.
BLIND JORDAN:	How do you know that?
WEEDY:	Because you're a slewfoot! All you're good for is slewfootin' up an' down th' road lookin' for that woman.
BLIND JORDAN:	Maybe you're right.
WEEDY:	Ain't that I got nothin' against you personally.
BLIND JORDAN:	No, ma'm, I just make your eye jump.
WEEDY:	Best thing you can do is to leave poor Alberta alone.
BLIND JORDAN:	All right, Mrs. Warren, I'll stay away.
WEEDY:	As long as you're in th' neighborhood.
BLIND JORDAN:	I've worked all th' buildin's in this neighborhood. [*He rises, moves to door.*] Goodbye, Mrs. Warren.
WEEDY:	Goodbye, Mr. Jordan. You will keep your promise?
BLIND JORDAN:	[*At door*] I won't bother Alberta no more.
WEEDY:	You've done a ole woman a great kindness.
BLIND JORDAN:	Yes'm.

[DOC *enters.*]

DOC:	Hello, Jordan.
BLIND JORDAN:	Doc? How are you?
DOC:	O.K.
BLIND JORDAN:	You been ridin' that number?
DOC:	Tell you the truth, I only played it once.
BLIND JORDAN:	Came out last week.
DOC:	Yes, I know.
BLIND JORDAN:	Should've been on it. Was a good number.
DOC:	They're all good if they fall.
BLIND JORDAN:	It's gonna fall again in a little while.
DOC:	Triple zeros?
BLIND JORDAN:	I'm tellin' you.
DOC:	Why don't you get on it?
BLIND JORDAN:	Me?
DOC:	Your money is as good as anybody else's.
BLIND JORDAN:	Wouldn't ever fall for me.
DOC:	Y'mean if you had money on it, it wouldn't have fallen?
BLIND JORDAN:	I'm just not lucky. I can give other people numbers but they wouldn't fall for me.
DOC:	If a number falls, it falls.
BLIND JORDAN:	Not for me.
DOC:	Maybe I'm th' same way.
BLIND JORDAN:	No, it'll fall for you.
DOC:	If I get a few extra dollars, I'll put somethin' on it.
BLIND JORDAN:	You broke, Doc?
DOC:	Not broke, just fractured.
BLIND JORDAN:	You wear a hat?
DOC:	A derby.
BLIND JORDAN:	Take off your hat.
DOC:	My hat? [*Removes hat*]
BLIND JORDAN:	[*Feels for hat. Lowers his hand with hat in it to his pocket level.*] Here. [*He removes change from both pockets and pours it into* DOC'S *hat.*]
DOC:	What're you doin'?
BLIND JORDAN:	Fillin' your hat up with change.
DOC:	I can't take your money.
BLIND JORDAN:	I want you to get on triple zeros.
DOC:	[*Stunned*] Must be thirty or forty dollars here.

BLIND JORDAN:	Play it. Every day! You don't even have to box it. No matter what combination it falls in, you win.
DOC:	Wait a minute . . .
BLIND JORDAN:	See you, Doc . . . Mrs. Warren. [*He exits.*]

[DOC *watches* BLIND JORDAN *go. He moves through the living room to the kitchen.*]

WEEDY:	Can't you say good evenin' to folks before you head for th' jug?
DOC:	[*Pouring a drink*] Good evenin'.
WEEDY:	Breath strong enough now to knock down folks when you pass.
DOC:	You ready to go?
WEEDY:	I ain't goin' nowhere with you if you keep drinkin' that whiskey. Never will I ride in a car with a drunkard.
DOC:	You're gonna look mighty funny ridin' all th' way down to th' train station standin' on my runnin' board.
WEEDY:	You shouldn't be allowed behind th' wheel of a car. Weavin' in an' outta traffic like a wild cowboy. You are a menace to public safety.
DOC:	C'mon, you goin' to th' train station or not?
WEEDY:	I dunno if I want to ride in that ole car anyhow.
DOC:	What's wrong with my car?
WEEDY:	Nothin' . . . outside it's a rattle trap ole enough to have driven th' Lawd to th' last supper.
DOC:	Look, I ain't got all evenin'. You goin' to Montgomery or not?
WEEDY:	If th' gate keep swingin' in th' direction it's swingin' in, I'm goin'. However, if th' gate should decide to swing in another direction, I may haffta change my plans accordin'ly. Lawd, give me th' strength to endure.

THE STY OF THE BLIND PIG | 47

DOC:	Sister, not only will you endure but you will prevail.
WEEDY:	Would you mind takin' my bags into the bedroom. I've decided not to go.
DOC:	[*Coming into living room*] You're not goin'?
WEEDY:	Can't go off and leave Alberta here by herself. Y'know she ain't well.
DOC:	Maybe a little rest from you will be a tonic for her.
WEEDY:	[*She rises from rocking chair.*] 'Course, if you would come over here and stay while I'm gone . . .
DOC:	What for?
WEEDY:	To see after her. Come here, Brother.
DOC:	For what?
WEEDY:	Just come here. [*He comes forward to* WEEDY, *who pushes him into rocking chair.*] Now, I need somebody to take care of things while I'm gone. [*She rocks him in chair.*]
DOC:	What're you doin'?
WEEDY:	Just sit still and listen. I need somebody here to take my place while I'm gone.
DOC:	She don't need nobody to see about her.
WEEDY:	I say she does.
DOC:	[*Peering out of window*] What's goin' on over there?
WEEDY:	Where?
DOC:	Across th' street?
WEEDY:	What'd you see?
DOC:	A milk man. Now, what's a milk man doin' deliverin' milk this time of evenin'?
WEEDY:	That's their cloak.
DOC:	Who?
WEEDY:	Bright woman lives over there on th' first floor. That milk man is in an' outta there all times of day. Poor man out workin' like a dog . . . got two jobs . . . mornin' an' night.
DOC:	Y'mean th' poor man is out workin' like a

	dog on two jobs an' unbeknownst to him he's got another mule kickin' in his stall?
WEEDY:	I'd be willin' to get you a little somethin'.
DOC:	Pay me to stay over here while you're gone?
WEEDY:	A few dollars.
DOC:	What's a few?
WEEDY:	More than you got.
DOC:	Before or after you go to Montgomery?
WEEDY:	When I come back.
DOC:	Your memory about money matters ain't too good.
WEEDY:	Whatever I have when I get back.
DOC:	[*Getting up out of rocking chair*] Naw, I got my own personal life to think about. Pearl keeps me pretty busy.
WEEDY:	You still foolin' with that infant?

[ALBERTA *enters with stockings.*]

ALBERTA:	I had to go all the way to Forty-third Street to find your size.
DOC:	Coulda took your time. Weedy ain't goin' nowhere.
ALBERTA:	Not going?
WEEDY:	Ain't settled in my mind that I oughta go.
ALBERTA:	[*Taking stocking out of box and taking off* WEEDY's *shoes*] Mama, you're getting on that train.
WEEDY:	I ain't made up my mind yet.
ALBERTA:	Way you done worried me about going . . . now, you're sure gonna go.
WEEDY:	Don't be so rough! You're gonna run th' stockin's.
ALBERTA:	Get her suitcase, Uncle Doc.
WEEDY:	You're just gonna make me go.
ALBERTA:	That's right.
DOC:	[*At door with suitcase*] Saint Weedy! Will you start marchin'!
WEEDY:	[*Reluctantly*] Well . . . [*Moving to door*]
ALBERTA:	[*Hands her coat*] Take this on your arm.

THE STY OF THE BLIND PIG | 49

WEEDY:	[*Taking coat*] Lawd willin', I should be back sittin' at my window two weeks from this very day. I'll send you a telegram and you an' Brother can pick me up.
DOC:	[*He has exited and is calling to her.*] C'mon, Weedy!
WEEDY:	I'll send you a picture postcard from Montgomery. That is, if I get to th' train in one piece. Should get it in a day or so.
DOC:	[*Off stage*] Weedy!
WEEDY:	[*Kisses* ALBERTA *on the cheek*] Be a good girl. Pray for me, I'm off with th' drunkard. [*Exits. From off stage*] C'mon an' make haste. I got a train to catch.
ALBERTA:	Jesus? [*She turns off the lights in apartment and moves to rocking chair and looks out of window.*]
BLIND JORDAN:	[*From the street below*] Amazing Grace how sweet it sounds It saved a wretch like me. I once was lost but now am found Was blind but now I see . . .
ALBERTA:	Jordan! [*Raises window and yells out*] Jordan!!
BLIND JORDAN:	Thro' many dangers, toils and snares I've already come It's Grace who's brought me safe thus far And Grace will lead me home . . .
ALBERTA:	Jordan!! . . . Can't you hear me calling you? Jordan!!!

[*The lights fade with* ALBERTA *at window.*]

SCENE 2

The sound of the CHOIR *from the little storefront church is heard in the blackout. A thin blue light rises on the half-open window in the living room. Slowly the light widens to envelop the entire apartment.* ALBERTA *and* BLIND JORDAN *are revealed sitting at the kitchen table.*

CHOIR: [*Off stage*]
Father alone understands why
Father alone knows all about it
Cheer up, my mother, walk in the sunshine
You'll understand it all by and by . . .

BLIND JORDAN: Where's that singin' comin' from?

ALBERTA: That little storefront church down the street.

[*The singing has faded into a hum.*]

BLIND JORDAN: They sing pretty fair.

ALBERTA: Why . . . why didn't you answer me when I called you?

BLIND JORDAN: I reckon I didn't hear you.

ALBERTA: You didn't hear me calling you from the window?

BLIND JORDAN: I reckon not.

ALBERTA: I ran down the street calling after you and and you just kept right on walking.

BLIND JORDAN: There was a lotta noise.

ALBERTA: Where were you going?

BLIND JORDAN: No place in particular . . . just goin'.

ALBERTA: You were . . . going away, weren't you? You were just going to walk away without even saying goodbye to me.

BLIND JORDAN: I promised Mrs. Warren . . .

THE STY OF THE BLIND PIG | 51

ALBERTA:	Mama? What did you promise Mama?
BLIND JORDAN:	That I wouldn't be hangin' around here while she's gone.
ALBERTA:	Don't pay Mama any attention.
BLIND JORDAN:	She's right. Shouldn't be hangin' round you.
ALBERTA:	I don't want you to go away, Jordan.
BLIND JORDAN:	You don't know anything about me, Alberta.
ALBERTA:	I don't need to know anything about you. I just don't want you to go away.
BLIND JORDAN:	I can't stay here forever. Been down here too long as it is. Done been through all the buildin's on this block twice. It's time for me to be movin' on.
ALBERTA:	You don't haffta do that. You could stay here.
BLIND JORDAN:	With you?
ALBERTA:	Be better than walking around begging.
BLIND JORDAN:	How could I keep lookin' for Grace and stay here with you at the same time?
ALBERTA:	You couldn't.
BLIND JORDAN:	You want me to stop looking for Grace?
ALBERTA:	You're never going to find her, Jordan.
BLIND JORDAN:	Doesn't make much difference whether I do or not.
ALBERTA:	Then why do you keep looking for her?
BLIND JORDAN:	Because that's what I do.
ALBERTA:	Why?
BLIND JORDAN:	I dunno any more. Maybe I did when I first started . . . but if I did, I've forgotten. Just seems like I gotta keep lookin' for her. Don't matter none if I find her or not. So long as I keep lookin' for her.
ALBERTA:	So you're gonna spend the rest of your days smelling up behind a woman that you ain't never gonna find.
BLIND JORDAN:	Maybe so.
ALBERTA:	Wouldn't it be better living here with me than stumbling by yourself?
BLIND JORDAN:	You're askin' me to live with you?
ALBERTA:	[After a moment] Yes . . .

BLIND JORDAN:	For how long?
ALBERTA:	No special time.
BLIND JORDAN:	But there would be a special time. One day that time would come. Then I'd be back lookin' for Grace again. One day I'd hear it in your voice.
ALBERTA:	Hear what in my voice?
BLIND JORDAN:	That special time.
ALBERTA:	I don't understand what you're saying.
BLIND JORDAN:	There's been other women who I've stopped with while I've been lookin' for Grace. Women that had soft, sweet voices. And so I stopped off. Their voice would be little . . . inside of them. After I was there a while I could hear their voices gettin' bigger and bigger. And for a while they would still be sweet . . . but then they would get hard and cracked. Then I would know it would be time for me to move on again. I would be back on the road lookin' for Grace. I don't think I can stop again.
ALBERTA:	You're saying that one day I would ask you to leave?
BLIND JORDAN:	Not in words.
ALBERTA:	You're wrong, Jordan, I wouldn't do that.
BLIND JORDAN:	You need somethin' from me . . . and I'd give it to you. But after a while you wouldn't need me any more.
ALBERTA:	What is it you think I need?
BLIND JORDAN:	Somebody . . .
ALBERTA:	You're wrong. I don't need anyone.
BLIND JORDAN:	You don't have to lie. It ain't nothin' to be ashamed about. It's nature. Ev'rybody got nature of one kind or another.
ALBERTA:	You think I'm talking about nature? You think that's why I want you to stay here? Because of nature?
BLIND JORDAN:	Ain't a thing wrong with that.
ALBERTA:	I don't have any nature.
BLIND JORDAN:	All right.
ALBERTA:	If you think that's why I wanted you to

	stay, you can get out of here right now. That's the only thing that's ever on men's minds. Mama's right. Men are lower than dogs!
BLIND JORDAN:	Maybe I better go.
ALBERTA:	Maybe you better. [*He rises. She touches his hand.*] Don't go, Jordan . . . I don't want you to go.
BLIND JORDAN:	I don't like a whole lotta fussin'.
ALBERTA:	I won't fuss. I promise. I won't fuss.
BLIND JORDAN:	[*Sitting back down*] If I'm gonna upset you . . .
ALBERTA:	I'm not upset. [*There is a long silence.*] I'm not going to let myself get upset.
BLIND JORDAN:	Naw, don't let yourself get upset.
ALBERTA:	[*After a pause*] I should have gone to church tonight.
BLIND JORDAN:	Why didn't you?
ALBERTA:	I dunno. I haven't been going too much lately. I guess they'll start thinking I've backslid.
BLIND JORDAN:	Have you backslid?
ALBERTA:	No, of course not. I'm still saved. After Emanuel Fisher's funeral I haven't been goin' too much.
BLIND JORDAN:	Who was he?
ALBERTA:	Just a boy . . . man . . . around the church.
BLIND JORDAN:	Was he a friend of yourn?
ALBERTA:	No . . . no. I admired him from afar.
BLIND JORDAN:	Never got close to him.

[*She rises, gets herself a drink.*]

ALBERTA:	You want a little taste?
BLIND JORDAN:	No, thank y'.
ALBERTA:	What was she like?
BLIND JORDAN:	Grace?
ALBERTA:	You know who I mean.
BLIND JORDAN:	What's to say?
ALBERTA:	Was she pretty?
BLIND JORDAN:	Folks said she was.

ALBERTA:	Was she nice?
BLIND JORDAN:	She had a nice voice.
ALBERTA:	What kinda voice is that?
BLIND JORDAN:	Raindust.
ALBERTA:	Raindust?
BLIND JORDAN:	Sorta made you feel . . . Did you ever smell raindust?
ALBERTA:	I don't even know what it is.
BLIND JORDAN:	Down home when it gets scratchin' hot. So hot you can't stand it any more . . . Then when it rains . . . folks down there call it th' white rain—hard, heavy, coolin' rain you can smell. Like th' ole earth is reborn. Fresh as the mornin' it was created.
ALBERTA:	That's what she was like?
BLIND JORDAN:	To me.
ALBERTA:	Did she have a lot of nature?
BLIND JORDAN:	She had a sufficient amount.
ALBERTA:	[*Pours another shot*] I shouldn't have asked you that. None of my business.
BLIND JORDAN:	Doesn't bother me.
ALBERTA:	[*After a moment*] Was she good up under her dress?
BLIND JORDAN:	Yes, she was. She was very good up under her dress.
ALBERTA:	What's wrong with me? What am I saying things like this for? I sound like some ole street woman.
BLIND JORDAN:	You're not a street woman.
ALBERTA:	I sound like one.
BLIND JORDAN:	No, you're not.
ALBERTA:	[*After a moment*] Did you ever think . . . that maybe Grace Waters might be dead?
BLIND JORDAN:	She ain't dead.
ALBERTA:	How can you be sure?
BLIND JORDAN:	If anything had happened to her—I'd know it. I couldn't go on lookin' for her and she . . . Why are you tryin' to put that idea in my head?
ALBERTA:	It's possible.
BLIND JORDAN:	It ain't possible.

THE STY OF THE BLIND PIG | 55

ALBERTA:	Is she too good to die?
BLIND JORDAN:	Yes! Yes, she is.
ALBERTA:	That's what they said about Emanuel Fisher. Said he was too good to die. Everybody loved him because he was so good. But that didn't stop him from falling out of the sky.
BLIND JORDAN:	He fell out of the sky?
ALBERTA:	He was learning to be a pilot. First time he went up by himself—the plane crashed. They had to cut him out of the wreckage. Then they had to cut the metal out of his body. He was so good. He was too good to die. And he had a voice that would make the very angels in heaven weep when he raised his voice in song. Yet God saw fit to let him die. 'S wonder the weeping Purple Angels didn't just swoop down and lift him out of that plane and bring him safely to the ground. Yes, Jesus, yes, Lord . . . he was so good.
BLIND JORDAN:	I suppose you went to his funeral.
ALBERTA:	Yes, Lord, yes, Jesus, I was there. . . . It was the biggest funeral in the history of the church . . . [*The lights in the apartment fade on* BLIND JORDAN *and plunge the whole apartment into darkness. A thin white light raises on* ALBERTA.] That place was really packed. They had to rent extra chairs for the people to sit down. And even in the streets, outside the church, people were standing. They came from all over Chicago to say one last goodbye to Emanuel Fisher—he was so beloved.

[*The sound of the* CHOIR *is heard.*]

CHOIR:	Father alone understands why Father alone knows all about it
ALBERTA:	And they really put him away in style. His mother and father must have spent every penny they had putting him away.

CHOIR:	Cheer up, my brother, don't you be sad
	You'll understand all by and by . . .
ALBERTA:	He had a beautiful powder-blue casket, lined with gentle white satin that shined like mirrors. And you never saw so many white roses in your life.
CHOIR:	Father alone knows all about it
	Father alone understands why . . .
ALBERTA:	There were thousands and thousands of white roses covering his powder-blue casket. And his casket was placed so it caught the light from the stained-glass window. The light, the yellow light fell on his face. . . . He looked so much like Jesus. Like a beautiful, sleeping Jesus. They didn't need to paint his face—he was beautiful without makeup.
CHOIR:	Cheer up, my mother, walk in the sunshine
	You'll understand all by and by . . .
ALBERTA:	He was even more beautiful in death than he had been in life. [CHOIR *is humming "Father Alone."*] The goodness still shined from his face. Then Reverend Goodlow stood up and asked Agnes McLoy to sing "Precious Lord." "Do it once more for Emanuel, Sister Agnes."
SOUND OF A WOMAN'S VOICE:	Precious Lord, take my hand
	Lead me on, let me stand . . .
ALBERTA:	[*Quietly*] Yes, Lord.
SOUND OF WOMAN'S VOICE:	I am weak, I am worn, I am tired
	Through the night, through the storm . . .
ALBERTA:	Yes, Jesus!
SOUND OF WOMAN'S VOICE:	Lead me on to the light
	Precious Lord, take my hand.
ALBERTA:	Then I had to read the telegrams.

[*Sound of* WOMAN *and* CHOIR *humming "Precious Lord"*]

THE STY OF THE BLIND PIG | **57**

ALBERTA: To the bereaved parents of Emanuel Fisher. Our heartfelt sympathy. Signed, The Reverend Lloyd S. Peters, Clarksdale, Mississippi. To Mr. and Mrs. Joseph Fisher. Our hearts share with you the tragedy of your loss. Signed, The Reverend Doctor John Thomas, 223 Decator Street, Cincinnati, Ohio. From Mr. and Mrs. John W. Lucas of Louisville, Kentucky, to the family of Emanuel Fisher. Please accept our deepest condolences at your loss. From Mr. and Mrs. Richard Matthew and family from Nashville, Tennessee. Our hearts reach out to you at this time of your great loss. To the family of Emanuel Fisher. Our deepest regrets at the passing of Emanuel Fisher. Dr. and Mrs. Harold H. Markus, Augusta, Georgia. [*The humming of "Precious Lord" fades.*] Emanuel Fisher was born in Clarksdale, Mississippi, on the sixth day of June in the year nineteen twenty-five. He was the son of Mr. Joseph Fisher and Marianne Lovelace Fisher. They traveled to Chicago in the year nineteen thirty-two when Emanuel Fisher was six years old. Mr. and Mrs. Joseph Fisher joined this church in the year of its dedication, which was spring of nineteen thirty-three. Emanuel Fisher attended Doolittle grammar school and Wendell Phillips High School, graduating with honors. The year after his graduation he entered Pickering College in the state of South Carolina. While there, he became active in the Christian Young People's Conference and won great recognition for his prize-winning speech, which was later published in the Christian Young People's Conference's annual magazine, called "The Flight of the Purple Angels." In his speech, "The Flight of the Purple Angels," he chose to reconcile life with death. He reminded those who were in the audience that day that we must not become too attached to this earthly life. That our lives here should be preparation for the life that is to come. For it is this life that is to come which is the reason for our being here. And we must earn that life . . . cleanse ourselves in order to earn that life. He tried to give the audience comfort in the knowledge that when the Heavenly Father calls us home we should not be afraid. For the Father has created an orchard for us to live in with life everlasting. That our labors in these vineyards down here is but a prelude to the rest we shall receive when the Purple Angels call us on our final journey. It is a journey that Emanuel Fisher, unlike most of us, looked forward to. Emanuel Fisher asked that when he began that last journey his loved ones and friends not mourn him. That they rejoice for he knows that he will be rejoicing in the bosom of our Savior, Jesus Christ. No, do not mourn Emanuel Fisher for he is this day sitting on the right hand of the Father, the Son and the Holy Ghost. Another has raised his voice in song this day. Another voice sings out with the Heavenly Host. We may not hear that voice because we are too far away. But the Purple Angels hear and they weep and are happy, for Emanuel Fisher flies with them.

VOICE OF
REVEREND GOODLOW: I wish to thank Sister Alberta for her words . . . [*The* CHOIR *sings softly "Just a Closer Walk with Thee."*] And I! AND I do not grieve, Emanuel Fisher.

ALBERTA: Yes, Jesus!

CHOIR: [*Softly*]

	Just a closer walk with thee
	Grant it, Jesus, if you please . . .
REVEREND GOODLOW:	For Emanuel Fisher has gone to Glory! Amen. I said Emanuel Fisher is sitting in glory . . .
ALBERTA:	Mercy, Jesus! Mercy!
REVEREND GOODLOW:	. . . for he has found life everlasting.

[CHOIR *is humming.*]

ALBERTA:	Oh, Jesus, have mercy! Jesus, have mercy!
REVEREND GOODLOW:	And even though his earthly body was twisted and mangled beyond repair . . . even though man with all his knowledge could not heal his body . . . even though they could not resurrect that body . . . Emanuel Fisher lives! For that motor is still running fine in glory. The breath of life has been blown back into our brother! The breath of life that only God can blow into him has been blown back into him.
ALBERTA:	Yes, Jesus, yes Lord!

[CHOIR: *humming.*]

REVEREND GOODLOW:	I can see him riding that train to glory! And Jesus is the conductor!
CONGREGATION:	Emanuel! Oh, Jesus, Emanuel!
REVEREND GOODLOW:	Tell them to get my throne ready, Emanuel! Tell them to get my crown ready, Emanuel! 'Cause I'm coming too!

[*Sounds of* CONGREGATION: *there are screams, moans and wails.*]

ALBERTA:	[*Being carried away*] Aw, Emanuel! Aw, Jesus. Glory! Take me too, Lord. I said take me too, Jesus!
REVEREND GOODLOW:	Tell them I'm coming too, Emanuel. Tell them to get my castle ready! Tell them to get my robes ready. Tell them I'm

coming, Emanuel, and I won't be long in getting there. I'm tired of this body! I'm tired of this strife! I'm tired, Emanuel! Whew. Oh, Lawd. How long!

ALBERTA: How long!!

CONGREGATION: How long!!!

REVEREND GOODLOW: How long, oh, Lord.

ALBERTA: How long, Jesus!

CONGREGATION: How long, Lord!!!

REVEREND GOODLOW: How long the night!

ALBERTA: Yes, Lord! Oh, yes, Lord!

CONGREGATION: Mercy, Lord! Lord, have mercy!

REVEREND GOODLOW: How long this darkness!

ALBERTA: [Falling to floor] I wanna shout Jesus! And dance! Amen! [Lies out on floor] Fill me with the Holy Ghost. Let me tremble with the Holy Ghost! [Her body trembling with the Holy Ghost. On her feet] Let me dance the dance of happiness! [The CHOIR still can be heard humming.] I want to dance the dance of happiness! [She goes into a wild, frenzied dance.] Let me speak in tongues, oh Lord. Twist my words into confusion, Jesus. Let the meaning of my words be withheld even from me. Only you, Jesus, and the beautiful Purple Angels understand my utterances. [Still dancing, she speaks gibberish.]

REVEREND GOODLOW: Amen!

CONGREGATION: Amen!!

ALBERTA: [Falls to floor] Amen. [She is on her knees.] Then they wheeled his body around for that last, final look. [Again the "Father Alone" is hummed by the CHOIR.] Oh, Jesus . . . [Screams] Emanuel! You're gone, Emanuel! Let me kiss you once. Never in life did I kiss you. Now in your never-ending sleep . . . I want to climb into the casket with you, Emanuel. [Slight pause] I'm soaking wet, Emanuel!

The sweat is pouring out of me! I want to climb in there with you and baptize you with my body fluids. Holy Ghost, take control over me. I can't control myself any more.

BLIND JORDAN: [*Out of the darkness*] Alberta!

[*The lights rise in the apartment.*]

ALBERTA: Oh, Lord!
BLIND JORDAN: [*Struggling to find her*] Alberta!
ALBERTA: [*She is at the couch on her knees.*] I want to kiss you again!
BLIND JORDAN: [*Finding her*] Stop it! Stop it, Alberta!
ALBERTA: [*Confused*] Emanuel?
BLIND JORDAN: [*Raising her to her feet*] Shhh! Shhh!
ALBERTA: I kissed you.
BLIND JORDAN: Yes.
ALBERTA: You're not Emanuel!
BLIND JORDAN: No.
ALBERTA: I want to kiss him one last, final time.
BLIND JORDAN: [*Embracing her*] No.
ALBERTA: You're not Emanuel.
BLIND JORDAN: I'm Jordan.
ALBERTA: Jordan?
BLIND JORDAN: The last of a long line of Blind Jordans.
ALBERTA: Jordan.
BLIND JORDAN: Shhh!
ALBERTA: Kiss me, Jordan. Please, kiss me.

[*He kisses her as the lights fade. The* CHOIR *from down the street rings out with* "*Father Alone.*"]

ACT III ● ● ●

SCENE 1

The light comes up on DOC *and* WEEDY, *alone in the apartment, at evening, several days later.* WEEDY *is seated at the window. She no longer rocks from the rhythm of the street below, but from a far-away interior rhythm that we cannot hear. She seems to have begun her process of withering away.* DOC *is in the kitchen, dressed in a brand-new gray pin-stripe suit and matching felt hat. He removes three bottles of whiskey from a brown paper bag, one of which he opens, and pours himself a drink.*

DOC: This may be the last drink I ever take in this house, Sister.

WEEDY: You done got your little money . . . gettin' ready to get on down th' road. I wouldn't expect you to stay here an' give me th' assistance I need.

DOC: I always said that when I hit th' number and got a few charlies in my pocket I'd be jumpin' back to Memphis.

WEEDY: Prosperity don't sit too well on some folks. Soon as they get a little money got, just go beside themselves, they commence to smell.

DOC: I'd rather have prosperity sit bad on me than have th' poor house sit good on me.

THE STY OF THE BLIND PIG | 63

WEEDY: Yes, sir, money done sure made a fool outta you. Done went out here and bought that little sweet water suit. Makes you look like you're seekin' employment on th' chain gang.

DOC: That's th' one thing I ain't seekin'—employment.

WEEDY: If you had anything in you at all you'd throw that money right in ole Jordan's face.

DOC: I can think of a whole lotta things I'd throw in somebody's face before money.

WEEDY: You ain't nothin', Brother. You just ain't nothin'. You ain't even much what th' birds left.

DOC: I wouldn't give you fifteen cents for all this ole random talk.

WEEDY: [Looks up to ceiling] I'd rather see her dead and in her grave than turn out this way.

DOC: Stop that, Weedy!

WEEDY: You approve of this kind of conduct?

DOC: I don't approve or disapprove.

WEEDY: No, because you been cloakin' for them right along.

DOC: I ain't cloakin' for nobody. She's a full-grown woman. If you don't like it, all I can say is—move out.

WEEDY: Think you're goin' down to Memphis and be the big shot again, don't y'? Folks down there done forget you ever existed in this world.

DOC: How they gonna forget me? They still remember Sportin' Jimmy Sweet, the Prince of Beale Street!

WEEDY: Folks done forgot you so long ago it ain't even funny.

DOC: They ain't forgot me.

WEEDY: Just wait till you get on down there. You'll see. May as well stay here and help me. You ain't never done nothin' for her.

DOC: [*Her last remark strikes deep.*] Why did you have to come back? If you had stayed the allotted time out, Jordan might have been gone. Why did you have to come back?

WEEDY: Couldn't stay down there.

DOC: I put you on th' train to Montgomery. You were suppose to stay for two weeks. But you had to bring your behind back and catch 'em.

WEEDY: That wasn't th' convocation I usta know. No sir, Jesus, it wasn't. It wasn't no more th' convocation I usta know than my big toe is.

DOC: Couldn't you have just stayed down there for the whole time?

WEEDY: Them colored folks done gone crazy down there in Montgomery. They had turned that whole convocation all th' way 'round. Had to walk ev'rywhere . . . tellin' colored folks not to ride th' buses. I tell you I don't know what done got into them folks. I had to walk so much my feet was just about to kill me.

DOC: Why wouldn't they ride the buses?

WEEDY: Lawd, don't start me to lyin'. Some young preacher got 'em all stirred up—raisin' sand. They just push out the regular folks at th' convocation. They came into one of our meetin's hollerin' they didn't wanna hear no more fogeyism. Young folk. The mess ain't even wiped good from their behinds an' they're callin' folks fogies. Tellin' folks not to ride th' bus cause they didn't want to sit in th' back.

DOC: People stir up ev'ry once in a while. Ain't nothin' to all that.

WEEDY: They say they gonna carry it all over th' South.

DOC: Carry what all over th' South?

WEEDY: Not ridin' th' buses.

DOC: Let th' fools walk if they don't want to ride.

WEEDY: Bound you it will be in Memphis by th' time you get there.

DOC: Now, how is it gonna be Memphis?

WEEDY: I heard a woman say that when she got to Memphis she was gonna start tryin' to get th' colored folks there not to ride th' buses.

DOC: They better keep that foolishness away from Memphis. If they know like I know, they better. Why can't folks leave things alone? Stirrin' up things . . .

WEEDY: That's why you better stay right on up here in Chicago. There's gonna be a whole lotta troubles down home.

DOC: Not in Memphis.

WEEDY: Didn't I just get through tellin' you . . .

DOC: Them folks come to Memphis with their foolishness and ain't nobody gonna pay them bit more 'tention. They better keep their behinds outta Memphis if they know what's good for 'em. We ain't never had no trouble down there and there sure ain't gonna be none now. Memphis is a sportin' town. It ain't got no time for no mess. Folks is out lookin' to have a good time.

WEEDY: You just go on back down there and see. You'll be right back up here directly.

DOC: Naw, I ain't never comin' back to Chicago. Not in this life anyhow. [*There is a pause. He looks at* WEEDY, *who turns away and looks out of window.*] We're just about th' last ones left, Sister.

WEEDY: Yeap—th' last ones left.

DOC: [*Moves toward her*] Sister . . .

WEEDY: Brother! [*As he is moving toward her*] Don't kiss me! We ain't never been a kissin' set of folks.

DOC: [*Retreating*] Naw, we never were a kissin' set of folks.

[*They both are frozen in place as a key is heard in the door.* ALBERTA *enters and comes into living room.*]

ALBERTA: Hello, Uncle Doc.

DOC: [*After a moment*] Ain't you two speakin'?

ALBERTA: She doesn't speak to me.

DOC: You two are sittin' up here in this house not speakin' to each other?

ALBERTA: [*Goes into kitchen*] I'll speak to her when she speaks to me.

DOC: [*Coming into kitchen*] I don't approve of this, Alberta. Not speaking to your mother.

ALBERTA: What'd you want me to do? I've tried to talk to her but she won't answer me. Looks at me like something dirty lying in the street.

DOC: Kinda of a shock to come home an' find you . . .

ALBERTA: Layin' up with a man I ain't married to.

DOC: Your mama don't believe in that sorta thing. It ain't a nice thing to do.

ALBERTA: You got a lot of nerve, Uncle Doc. After all the women you've laid around with in your life.

DOC: But they weren't my flesh and blood.

ALBERTA: What about Mama?

DOC: What about her?

ALBERTA: You think I don't know?

DOC: [*Takes out his watch*] Listen, I've got to pick up Pearl . . . get my suitcase.

ALBERTA: You're not driving?

DOC: No, I sold my car. Remember—she's your mother.

ALBERTA: I remember. Oh, yes, I remember. [*She follows him to door.*]

THE STY OF THE BLIND PIG | 67

DOC: I'll stop back by on my way to the train station. [*He exits.*]

[ALBERTA *looks at* WEEDY, *who is ignoring her.*]

ALBERTA: Mama . . .
WEEDY: I been 'buked and I been scorned
I been 'buked and I been scorned . . .
ALBERTA: Mama . . . I have to talk to you.
WEEDY: Jesus died to set me free . . .
ALBERTA: [*Gets an envelope out of her purse*] Mama, we have to move. Here's a letter from the city. Says this building has been condemned and they are going to tear it down.
WEEDY: I been 'buked and I been scorned
I been 'buked and I been scorned . . .
ALBERTA: Mama, you're gonna have to loan me the money to find another apartment.
WEEDY: I ain't got no money.
ALBERTA: Mama, you've got some money.
WEEDY: All I got is my little pension money. And I give that to Reverend Goodlow to put in my burial policy.
ALBERTA: We'll have to cash it in.
WEEDY: Cash it in! No, sir, Jesus!
ALBERTA: Mama, we have to move! They are going to tear the building down. Do you understand? This building has been condemned!
WEEDY: I been 'buked and I been scorned
I been 'buked and I been scorned . . .
ALBERTA: We can't stay here. Mama, you don't have to stay here. Papa is not coming back.
WEEDY: I ain't waitin' for him to come back! I wish that thing would come steppin' up here after he ran off. I'd set his soul to rest. I'd spit in his face! Ev'rytime that thing crosses my mind I get mad!
ALBERTA: You silly ole woman!
WEEDY: Let me tell you somethin', heifer! If you

don't know who you foolin' with, you better ask somebody. Don't you be hollerin' at me. 'Cause I'll lay you cold as a milkshake! And you needn' be rollin' your eyes and pokin' out your mouth like you don't like it. And if you don't like it, smile and play like you do. An' you needn' be lookin' like you're gettin' ready to try me. 'Cause if you do, I'll hurt you.

ALBERTA: I'm not getting ready to try you.

WEEDY: I know you ain't. Unless you done lost your mind.

ALBERTA: I'm trying to explain to you we have to move.

WEEDY: [*Rises and goes into her bedroom*] I reckon I'll lie down.

ALBERTA: Mama, the building is condemned!

WEEDY: What you hollerin' about, heifer? I ain't deaf. Ain't you got sense enough to know I hear you? [*Exits into bedroom, closing the door*]

ALBERTA: [*Flops down on couch*] That woman's gonna worry me to . . . [*She cups her hand over her mouth. Fade out.*]

SCENE 2

The lights fade in about an hour later. ALBERTA *and* JORDAN *are seated on the couch, dressed in their coats.* WEEDY, *also dressed in her coat, is seated at the window.*

ALBERTA: What time did Uncle Doc say he'd be coming back? Mama? [WEEDY *does not answer.*] If he doesn't hurry up, he'll be done missed his train.

BLIND JORDAN: What time does his train leave?

ALBERTA: Ten-thirty.

BLIND JORDAN: What time is it now?

ALBERTA: About nine.

BLIND JORDAN: Still got an hour and a half.

WEEDY: [*After a long pause*] Mr. Jordan?

BLIND JORDAN: Yes, ma'm.

ALBERTA: Mama, don't start.

WEEDY: I ain't startin' nothin'. I just want to ask Mr. Jordan a question.

BLIND JORDAN: What is it, Mrs. Warren?

WEEDY: Are you plannin' to vacate th' premises anytime soon or have you decided to make this your permanent headquarters?

ALBERTA: Mama!

WEEDY: I only want to know so I can make my plans accordingly.

ALBERTA: He doesn't have to answer you anything.

BLIND JORDAN: Mrs. Warren? What is it you really want to know?

ALBERTA: You don't have to answer her. Don't pay her any attention Jordan. [*To* WEEDY] Why do you always have to keep up the devil?

BLIND JORDAN:	What is it you want Alberta to know, Mrs. Warren?
WEEDY:	[*After a pause*] How many, do you reckon, red-light houses you done played your music box in, Mr. Jordan?
ALBERTA:	Red-light houses . . .
BLIND JORDAN:	What do you know about red-light houses?
WEEDY:	I done covered a whole lotta road.
ALBERTA:	You played in red-light houses?
BLIND JORDAN:	Quite a few.
ALBERTA:	Red-light houses!
BLIND JORDAN:	I was born in a red-light house. The same house—same room—exact same bed my father was born in. A place called the Sty of the Blind Pig.
WEEDY:	A house down in New Orleans. He's got the smell of blood on him, Alberta. I could smell it the minute he walked into this house.
ALBERTA:	How do you know so much about it?
WEEDY:	Sure as I'm sittin' here he's got th' smell of blood on him.
BLIND JORDAN:	She's right—I do have the smell of blood on me. The smell of butchered pig. That smell gets into your pores—can't wash it off.
ALBERTA:	I don't smell anything.
BLIND JORDAN:	I can smell it on myself! The smell of the bowels of the pig. All the parts that the others threw away were brought to the sty and cooked in scaldin'-hot water. Sometimes that hot water got thrown into someone's face. You ever hear a man's scream when he had been scalded by the hot water where the pig had been cooked in? It started with the butchering of th' pig . . . men died in th' Sty of the Blind Pig. So did women.
ALBERTA:	What kind of women?
BLIND JORDAN:	Women who sold their bodies in the Sty

THE STY OF THE BLIND PIG | 71

of the Blind Pig. Women who carried knives and cut their pimps when the shame overtook them. And pimps who cut up their women because they had lost their manhood. I've played my music box in places where men and women stood toe to toe and cut each other to pieces while cursin' their own mothers for birthin' them into this world. They've fallen on me with th' blood just oozin' out of them. And I could smell th' flesh of th' pig that had mixed in with their blood.

ALBERTA: You're making this up.

BLIND JORDAN: An' th' ones that was left from Saturday night got up on Sunday mornin' an' went to church to pray for those that had been slaughtered th' night before.

ALBERTA: She told you to say all this, didn't she?

WEEDY: I ain't told him nothin'.

ALBERTA: Lies! You're making this all up! Why, Jordan? Because you want to go back and hunt for Grace Waters again!

BLIND JORDAN: [*Raises his shirt*] Makin' it up! Haven't you seen this?

WEEDY: Look like somebody tried to cut your guts out.

BLIND JORDAN: Ain't you seen it?

ALBERTA: No! And I don't want to see it!

BLIND JORDAN: Look at it.

ALBERTA: Put your shirt down!

BLIND JORDAN: How could you lay up with me and not see it?

ALBERTA: I've never noticed it.

BLIND JORDAN: You want to know how I got it?

ALBERTA: No!

BLIND JORDAN: A woman gave it to me.

WEEDY: What woman?

ALBERTA: I don't want to hear about it.

WEEDY: What woman put her mark on you, Mr. Jordan?

BLIND JORDAN:	A woman that I killed. I choked her to death as she tried to cut me to death.
ALBERTA:	Then why ain't you in jail?
BLIND JORDAN:	There ain't no punishment for killin' a nigger woman on Saturday night. You just go to church on Sunday mornin' an' pray.
WEEDY:	This is what you been layin' up here with! This is what you brought into th' house.
ALBERTA:	You any better than he is!
WEEDY:	What?
ALBERTA:	Running down to the church carrying on with Reverend Goodlow.
WEEDY:	What are you talkin' about?
ALBERTA:	You been going with him for over forty years.
WEEDY:	Where did you get that from?
ALBERTA:	Why do you think Papa ran off?
WEEDY:	Because he didn't have no grit in his craw.
ALBERTA:	He found out about you and Reverend Goodlow.
WEEDY:	That fool's accused me of havin' Reverend Goodlow before we even much left th' South. Reverend Goodlow was pastorin' a church down there and he swore up and down that I was messin' around with him.
ALBERTA:	And you kept on when you got up here.
WEEDY:	I didn't even know that man was in Chicago when we moved up here. Did that thing tell you all of this?
ALBERTA:	Everybody around that church knows it. I guess Papa got tired of everybody pointing at him like he was a fool.
WEEDY:	That ain't why he ran off.
ALBERTA:	I know better.
WEEDY:	He ran off because he didn't believe that you were his.
ALBERTA:	Didn't believe I was his.
WEEDY:	Kept accusin' me of Reverend Goodlow for so long he commence to see him in you.

ALBERTA:	You're a liar!
WEEDY:	Don't you call me no liar! I bound I'll slap you clear into next week. Your daddy with his ole strange ways . . . Never did think he could make no baby. When I was carryin' you he use to holler that he was too weak to make a baby.
ALBERTA:	Was I . . . ?
WEEDY:	What?
ALBERTA:	Was I his?
WEEDY:	You better get away from me!
ALBERTA:	Tell me the truth.
WEEDY:	[*Sits down*] Go on away from me, gal, before I knock you clear into next week.
ALBERTA:	[*Looks at* BLIND JORDAN, *then at* WEEDY] I wish that I had never laid eyes on either one of you two. What's that Sister Martin always hollers out? How long! How long, oh Lord! How long!
BLIND JORDAN:	Alberta?
ALBERTA:	Don't come near me, please.
BLIND JORDAN:	That life is gone. They done tore down th' Sty of the Blind Pig. Even th' blind street singers are dyin' out.
ALBERTA:	Let them all die out. Let us all die out. Make room for somebody else. The sooner the better.

[*There is a pause.*]

DOC:	[*Off stage*] Hey, y'all! [*Bangs on door*]
ALBERTA:	[*She opens door.*] It's Uncle Doc. [DOC *enters. He is in a state of shock. His face is swollen and bloody and his clothes have been torn.*] What happen to you?
WEEDY:	Brother!
DOC:	[*Moves to couch*] They jumped me!
BLIND JORDAN:	What is it? What's wrong?
WEEDY:	[*Coming to couch*] What happen to you?
DOC:	They tried to rob me.
WEEDY:	Who tried to rob you?

DOC: Pearl and some young cat. Tried to take my money away from me. Threw me down th' stairs.

ALBERTA: They get it?

DOC: [*Almost breaking*] I woulda shared it with her. I would have taken her back to Memphis with me. She woulda been somebody down there with me. [*Pause*] I sure don't think she'd do me thataway. Wish I never had hit th' numbers. Rather not have hit them than have her do this to me. Them goddamn triple zeros!

WEEDY: You're gonna destroy us all, Mr. Jordan.

[*Fade out*]

SCENE 3

The lights come up several hours later. The apartment is dark and empty. We hear the sound of the key in the lock. WEEDY *enters followed by* ALBERTA.

WEEDY: Mr. Jordan? [*Snaps on light*] Mr. Jordan?

ALBERTA: I told you he wouldn't be here.

WEEDY: Maybe he got lost in th' train station. He was standin' right next to me when you went off to get th' magazines for Brother. I looked around an' he was gone. Well, maybe he'll make it back all right.

ALBERTA: I told you he's not coming back.

WEEDY: Did you tell him not to come back?

ALBERTA: No.

WEEDY: But you know he's not comin' back.

ALBERTA: Yes. [*There is a pause.*] Was he ever really here?

WEEDY: Huh?

ALBERTA: I was just wonderin' something out loud.

WEEDY: What was that?

ALBERTA: Just something that passed through my mind.

WEEDY: [*After a pause*] Well, Brother's ridin' now.

ALBERTA: Riding south.

WEEDY: I wonder where all them young folks was goin'?

ALBERTA: Young folks?

WEEDY: Didn't you see 'em? Got on th' same train with Brother. Lord, they sure looked a mess. Ev'ryone of 'em had nappy hair.

ALBERTA: Nappy hair?

WEEDY: Look like they woulda gone to th' beauty parlor an' got their hair straighten 'fore they went off visitin'.

ALBERTA: Yes, I saw them. They did all have nappy hair, didn't they? Funny, I didn't even think about it until you brought it up. But now that you mention it . . .

WEEDY: Lord, never would I go off travelin' with my head lookin' like that.

ALBERTA: Sometimes I wish that I hadn't started straightening mine. Maybe it wouldn't be half burned out now. [*She moves to window and sits in rocking chair.*]

WEEDY: Y'know somethin'—I was thinkin'. You look for another place. I'll talk to . . . Reverend Goodlow and maybe I can draw out somethin' on my funeral savin's plan.

ALBERTA: You don't have to do that.

WEEDY: Well, if they're condemnin' th' buildin' . . .

ALBERTA: They probably won't be tearing it down for a little while yet.

WEEDY: Think we oughta wait until they commence to destroy it right over our heads?

ALBERTA: Ain't no need in getting in a rush now.

WEEDY: Think we got time?

ALBERTA: Time enough, I reckon.

WEEDY: Well, anythin' you want to do is all right with me.

ALBERTA: All right.

WEEDY: From here on in I guess everythin' is up to you.

ALBERTA: Up to me?

WEEDY: If you want to draw all the money out of the funeral plan—all right by me.

ALBERTA: Now you say that. After it's all over and done with you say that.

WEEDY: What's all over and done with?

ALBERTA: Everything.

WEEDY: I don't have the slightest idea of what you're talkin' about.

ALBERTA: Why don't you go to bed, Mama?

WEEDY: Yes, I am tired. [*Moves to door*] What did you mean? Everythin's all over and done with.

THE STY OF THE BLIND PIG | 77

ALBERTA:	You know what I mean, Mama.
WEEDY:	No, I don't.
ALBERTA:	You just think about it. Sleep on it. It'll come to you.
WEEDY:	Not tired as I am, I won't think about nothin'. All I want to do is lay my head down on that pillow.
ALBERTA:	Good night.
WEEDY:	Good night. [*She enters the bedroom.*]

[*The lights dim to suggest the passing of time.*]

ALBERTA:	[*Rocking at the window*] Well, sir, will you look at that. Look at her strut. Struttin' like she was th' best-lookin' thing on the street. [*She rises, raises window.*] Hey, you! Yes, I'm talkin' to you. You sure oughta go somewhere and take off that red dress and do somethin' about your behind shakin'. It's bouncing like a rubber ball. You needin' be tryin' to ignore me— you hear me! [*Sits down*] Lord, these young folks ain't a bit of count nowadays. They just ain't nothin'. They ain't even much what th' birds left. Like I was sayin' to Mama just th' other day . . . Mama! Mama? [*She rises and crosses to* WEEDY's *bedroom, opens door.*] Mama? Where are you, Mama? [*She goes into her own room.*] Mama . . . Come back, Mama! [*She comes back to window.*] Oh, Mama . . . you're layin' out there all by yourself. Mama!

[*The sound of a* CHOIR *is heard.*]

CHOIR:	Father alone knows all about it
	Father alone understands why
	Cheer up, my brother, walk in the sunshine

You'll understand all by and by . . .

ALBERTA: I'm all right, Mama! I'm all right! [CHOIR, *humming*.] Because I got grit in my craw. I got a whole lotta grit in my craw!

[*Fade out*]

AMERICAN NIGHT CRY
A Trilogy ● ● ● ● ●

THUNDER IN THE INDEX

● ● ● ● ● ● ● ● ●

"*Ay me, what act,*
That roars so loud, and Thunders
in the Index?

HAMLET, Act III, Scene IV

A *thin blue light rises on* JOSHUA NOON, *tied up in a red camisole, in the psychiatric ward of a city hospital. The bed is placed in the center of the stage facing the audience and has been placed on a platform which gives the effect of an altar. Cut high in the back wall is a small window, with either the early light of morning or the fading light of the evening coming through. There is a small chair at the left side of the bed. A few feet from the chair stands a screen. Down right is a door of steel bars. On the other side of the bars is a heavy black door which is now closed. The walls of the room are painted a dark color and seem almost purple. The set should not be realistic, but an outline.*

The sound of music is heard in the distance of JOSHUA's *mind. The music is the vigorous sound of drums chorused by chanting in a strange tongue. Slowly* JOSHUA *begins to regain his consciousness and discover himself in the strange room. The drums and the chants begin to fade away.*

JOSHUA: [*Lying flat on his back*] Water! Water! I wants some water! [*Pause*] I'm thirsty! . . . I wants some water. I want some nice cool water. [*Struggles in the camisole*] What? Hey? [*Struggles*] Help! Help me. . . . Help me, somebody. Somebody come and help me get out of this damn thing. Get this damn thing offa me. Please, someone come and help me out of this thing. Can anybody hear me? Will you please come and take this damn thing offa me. [*Pause, waits for answer*] If you don't want it ripped up, you better come and take it off me. [*Struggles to point of exhaustion*] Hey . . . somebody . . . come and get this thing offa me. . . .

[*The thick black door on the other side of the bars opens and* DOCTOR SAMUEL GOLDBERG *and* NURSE SALLY TOWERS *appear on the other side of the bars.* GOLDBERG *is a tall man of forty, dressed in a dark blue suit and black horn-rimmed glasses.* NURSE TOWERS *is a thin, very tall young woman, dressed in the traditional uniform, with an artificial smile on her face which seems to be hiding the very disturbed look in her eyes.*]

GOLDBERG: How's he been?
NURSE: [*Unlocking door*] Fine. Sleeping mostly.
GOLDBERG: [*Entering*] Call you if I need you, Nurse.
NURSE: [*Locking door behind him*] All right, Doctor.
JOSHUA: Water!
GOLDBERG: You want some water? [*He moves to table behind bed and picks up glass of water and holds glass to* JOSHUA*'s mouth. Places glass back on table and moves to foot of bed to examine chart.*]
JOSHUA: Thanks, baby.
GOLDBERG: [*Reading chart*] How'd you feel this morning, Joshua?
JOSHUA: A minute ago I felt like I was dyin'. Like I was bein' pulled away. Somewhere, far away. Cross a lotta water. Kept hearin' this music . . . played on a flute.
GOLDBERG: [*Takes out his pen*] What kind of music? What kind of music did you hear, Joshua? [*Writes on chart*] Do you like music, Joshua?

JOSHUA:	O.K., I guess.
GOLDBERG:	[*Still reading chart*] Jazz, I bet.
JOSHUA:	What makes you think I dig jazz, baby?
GOLDBERG:	Oh, I don't know. . . . Most people do, don't they?
JOSHUA:	Me, I dig classical music. Like I gas behind them cold sounds.
GOLDBERG:	I love jazz.
JOSHUA:	Like th' man said—to each his own when he kissed the cow's ass. [JOSHUA *tries to sit up in bed.*]
GOLDBERG:	[*Cranks bed*] Better?
JOSHUA:	Like lay it on me, man, what's this thing you got me tied up in?
GOLDBERG:	You were a little upset . . . when you were brought in and we didn't want you to do injury to yourself.
JOSHUA:	Man, like how'd you sound? Injure me? Last stud in this world I'd do injury to—is me. And you'd better believe me when I tell you, 'cause that's square business. Say, like pull my coat?
GOLDBERG:	Pull your coat?
JOSHUA:	Run it down to me, baby.
GOLDBERG:	Run it down?
JOSHUA:	Yeah, like pull my coat an' let me in on the happenin's. Who you suppose to be, baby?
GOLDBERG:	My name is Doctor Goldberg.
JOSHUA:	Had your nose fixed, huh?
GOLDBERG:	I beg your pardon.
JOSHUA:	That ain't the nose you were born with, is it?
GOLDBERG:	Why are you so concerned about my nose?
JOSHUA:	I ain't concerned. Just that I can tell one of them noses a mile away. They all look just alike.
GOLDBERG:	Now this music that you heard? Did you hear voices with the music?
JOSHUA:	I hear voices everyday of my life, man.
GOLDBERG:	Where do you hear these voices?
JOSHUA:	In space.

GOLDBERG: [*Writing*] In space? What do the voices say to you?

JOSHUA: They don't say nothin' . . . I just hear 'em. They're sounds, man.

GOLDBERG: What kind of sounds?

JOSHUA: Sounds of cats splittin' th' air as they try to fly across rooftops. An' th' sounds of cats slicin' their feet as they walk through streets of broken, jagged, sharp glass. An' I hear th' sound of them cats singin' as the liquid dreams flow through their veins. An' I can hear the sound of them cat's screams when they crash into them tall concrete buildings. An' I can hear the muffled whinin' of children who were born half dead walkin' around in stunted hollow bodies. An' I can hear gray, wrinkled-eyed old men who never heard th' sound of their balls ringin'. An' I can hear th' sounds of th' pimps tryin' to ring their padded balls an' pretendin' t' hear 'em. An' I hear the quiet orgasms of silent, tight-headed old women with Jesus's music playin' inside of them. You look at them an' you can see right through 'em . . . but they're there. You have to hear 'em to see 'em. They're there . . . transparent sounds clashin' in space.

GOLDBERG: Do the voices . . . sounds . . . ever speak directly to you, Joshua?

JOSHUA: You know what I'm talkin' about, don't you, chief? You know exactly what I'm talkin' about. You can turn yourself inside out tryin' to deny it, but you know.

GOLDBERG: You said sometimes you heard screams.

JOSHUA: I use to think I was th' only one in th' world that heard them sounds.

GOLDBERG: Can you describe these screams?

JOSHUA: Do you smother them out, my man?

GOLDBERG: You're not answering my questions.

NURSE: [*On other side of bars. She unlocks door,*

THUNDER IN THE INDEX | 87

	enters carrying a tray.] Is it all right, Doctor?
GOLDBERG:	Hungry, Joshua?
NURSE:	[*She places tray on stand next to bed.*] Bet he's almost starved to death. How do you feel this morning, Joshua? Better?
JOSHUA:	I feel like a letter in the post office waitin' t' be mailed. Hey, don't anybody around here call you Mr. Noon?
NURSE:	Doctor, shall I?
GOLDBERG:	Hmmm? Yes, I think maybe you better, Nurse.
NURSE:	[*Placing napkin around his neck*] So you're feeling better this morning, hey, Joshua?
JOSHUA:	Mr. Noon does not feel better this morning.
NURSE:	[*Smiles*] Sure you do.
JOSHUA:	If I'm so much outta my skull, I ain't got sense enough to know how I feel, what th' hell you askin' me for?
NURSE:	[*Holding milk to his mouth*] Now drink it down.
JOSHUA:	Ain't y' gonna take this thing offa me so I can eat?
GOLDBERG:	The nurse'll feed you, Joshua.
JOSHUA:	I don't need anybody to feed me. I know how to feed myself.
GOLDBERG:	I wish I had it so good. In bed with a beautiful nurse to feed me. See how well we treat you here.
NURSE:	Doctor . . . [*She moves downstage and motions for him to join her.*] may I speak to you a moment?
GOLDBERG:	[*Moving down toward her*] Yes.
NURSE:	Doctor . . . ? Sorry, Doctor, but I don't know your name.
GOLDBERG:	Goldberg, Samuel Goldberg.
NURSE:	Goldberg? Doctor Goldberg?
GOLDBERG:	Yes. Something wrong with my name?
NURSE:	No, of course not. It's just that . . .
GOLDBERG:	What?
NURSE:	I would have taken you for Irish or Italian.

GOLDBERG: Lot of people take me for Irish . . . or Italian.

NURSE: You don't look . . . Jewish.

GOLDBERG: I'm not really. I mean my mother and father were, but I'm not religious.

NURSE: Oh. Well, Doctor, we have a problem.

GOLDBERG: What kind of problem?

NURSE: We're missing a patient.

GOLDBERG: What?

NURSE: I went in to take 2A his breakfast and the door was open and he was gone.

GOLDBERG: How did this happen?

NURSE: I imagine one of the attendants was careless and didn't lock the door behind him. The only way I can account for it.

GOLDBERG: The floor door is kept locked, isn't it?

NURSE: Yes, but we can't find him. We searched every foot of the floor. The johns, the closets—everywhere.

GOLDBERG: Maybe he was released.

NURSE: We can't find any release on him.

GOLDBERG: All right, I'll look into it. You finish feeding Joshua and I'll check with admissions.

NURSE: All right, Doctor.

[GOLDBERG *moves to the door as the* NURSE *crosses back to* JOSHUA.]

JOSHUA: What were you two whispering about?

GOLDBERG: I'll see Joshua after you've fed him. [*Exits*]

NURSE: All right, Doctor.

JOSHUA: I asked you two what you were whisperin' about?

NURSE: [*Picking up glass of milk*] C'mon now, drink this down so I can get out of here.

JOSHUA: Look, chick, when I eat I feed myself.

NURSE: Do you want this milk?

JOSHUA: No, I don't want the milk.

NURSE: How about the prunes? Do you want the prunes?

JOSHUA: I ain't constipated.

NURSE: You want to eat, Joshua?

JOSHUA: Eat it yourself, chick. Prunes'll be good for you—you need 'em.

NURSE: [*Hiding her anger*] I'm here to help you.

JOSHUA: Then, would you please take this damn thing off me?

NURSE: That's up to the doctor.

JOSHUA: I want to get out of this damn thing!

NURSE: That must be the doctor's decision.

JOSHUA: I have to wait until the doctor decides.

NURSE: That's right, you'll have to wait for the doctor to decide.

JOSHUA: I have decided. I want to get out of this damn thing.

NURSE: You'll have to wait until the doctor gives the order.

JOSHUA: How would you like to be strapped up in this thing?

NURSE: If I thought it was doing me some good.

JOSHUA: You ever had one of these things on?

NURSE: Why?

JOSHUA: I'd just like to know.

NURSE: You're not here to interrogate me.

JOSHUA: When were you tied up in one of these things?

NURSE: What makes you think it has ever been necessary to place me under restraint?

JOSHUA: You mean you've never been placed under restraint, huh?

NURSE: No, of course not.

JOSHUA: Then how in the hell do you know how it feels?

NURSE: I didn't say I did.

JOSHUA: You said it was doing me good. Now, you go tell that doctor that I want this thing offa me.

NURSE: Don't you dare give me orders.

JOSHUA: Go tell that damn doctor I itch.

NURSE: If you tell me where you itch, I'll scratch you.

JOSHUA: Oh, you'll scratch me. O.K., scratch me.

NURSE:	Where do you itch?
JOSHUA:	On the most private parts of me.
NURSE:	You're a wise guy.
JOSHUA:	Piss off, Minnie Mouse.
NURSE:	[*Taking the tray*] What's that supposed to mean?
JOSHUA:	Anything you want it to mean. [*He watches her cross to the door.*] Oh, yeah, you lost somethin'.
NURSE:	[*At door with tray*] Huh?
JOSHUA:	Your smile. Maybe you dropped it down on the floor. Why don't you crawl around and look for it, Minnie Mouse?
NURSE:	I could call you a few names too, chum.
JOSHUA:	I'm not your chum.
NURSE:	I'll remember you at medication time. The longest, sharpest needles I can find. And I'm going to stick it right in your . . . [*As she concludes her speech,* GOLDBERG *appears on the other side of the door.* GOLDBERG *inspects tray.*]
GOLDBERG:	Did he take nourishment?
NURSE:	He was too busy giving me a hard time.
GOLDBERG:	Admission has no record of 2A being released. I want you to have the attendants make a complete search of the floor.
NURSE:	They already have, Doctor.
GOLDBERG:	Then let them make another one. I want every foot of the floor checked and checked again.
NURSE:	All right, Doctor . . . I'll get right to it. [*She exits through the door.*]
JOSHUA:	Hey, Cous . . .
GOLDBERG:	Cous?
JOSHUA:	You know what they say, chief. Niggers and Jews are first cousins. You believe that, chief, that you an' me'er first cousins? Hey, Cousin Goldberg?
GOLDBERG:	Doctor Goldberg.
JOSHUA:	You don't like being first cousin to a nigger, huh?

GOLDBERG:	[*Moving to chair*] Just take it easy, Joshua.
JOSHUA:	Down South they say Jews are niggers turned inside out. Do you believe that, chief? That Jews are niggers turned inside out?
GOLDBERG:	I don't care for that word.
JOSHUA:	You like "black bastard" better, huh?
GOLDBERG:	No, I don't like that either.
JOSHUA:	What about "coon"? "Spade"? "Spook"? "Boogie"? "Shine"? "Eightball"?
GOLDBERG:	I don't use that kind of language.
JOSHUA:	What's your word, chief?
GOLDBERG:	I don't have one.
JOSHUA:	You don't have one, my man?
GOLDBERG:	No, I don't. You've got a king-sized chip on your shoulder, haven't you?
JOSHUA:	Maybe if there weren't so many axes swinging, there wouldn't be so many chips flying.
GOLDBERG:	Feeling sorry for yourself isn't going to help much.
JOSHUA:	What should I do? Develop a sense of humor?
GOLDBERG:	That might be a great asset.
JOSHUA:	Man, step on me an' I'm gonna holler. I'll wake up th' world with my hollerin'. I'm gonna holler so loud I'll bust your eardrums.
GOLDBERG:	Is that what you want to do? Burst the eardrums of everyone?
JOSHUA:	Look, my man . . . Cousin Goldberg.
GOLDBERG:	I'm not your cousin, I'm your doctor.
JOSHUA:	Why don't you untie me and let me slip out of here?
GOLDBERG:	You were sent to us by the court for observation.
JOSHUA:	All you got to do is untie me and leave the door open.
GOLDBERG:	I'm afraid that that is impossible.
JOSHUA:	But Cous . . .
GOLDBERG:	I'm not your cousin. I'm your doctor. Do

you understand? You were sent to us for observation. That is the beginning and the end of any responsibility I have to you. The decision to either release you or hold you in incarceration is not mine to make. I will report the findings of my examination to the proper authorities along with my recommendations. But finally the disposition of your case is in the hands of the court. I have no personal interest in you or your color. That is not my function here. My function here is that of a doctor trying to do a job. I've taken too much of your abuse already. And I won't take one more word of it. Now, I'm a doctor! Your doctor! You will give me the respect that I am due. Do you understand? You're not to heap any more of your vile abuse on me. Now, you'd better get that clear and straight in your head if you know what's good for you.

JOSHUA: You threatenin' me, chief?

GOLDBERG: You're damn right I am.

JOSHUA: You got the advantage, chief. I'm all tied up.

GOLDBERG: That's right, chief. You're all tied up. You're tied up and I am free with the advantage and I'm going to keep it.

JOSHUA: You think you're in, don't you?

GOLDBERG: In what?

JOSHUA: 'Cause you got this little old chicken-shit job.

GOLDBERG: I'm a member of the staff of this institution.

JOSHUA: Man, if you don't sound like ole Harold.

GOLDBERG: Harold?

JOSHUA: My brother—fifteen-thousand-dollars-a-year Harold and his bitch-wife have a combined income of twenty-five thousand dollars a year. They are both members of staff in institutions. Harold and his bitch-wife live in a middle-income, interracial housin' project . . . only they call it a "development" instead of a "project." And they have cock-tails before dinner. Both he and his bitch-wife and their reality-coping children have analysts. And their analyst's a staff member somewhere in some institution. The bitch-wife put Harold up to getting an unlisted telephone number so he can't be gotten in touch with. Whenever I want to see Harold and his bitch-wife and their stingy-face children, who are always copin' with reality, I have to write him a letter. An' it can't be longer than one page an' statin' th' reason that I want to see him an' the exact day an' time I would like to see him. Then they take my letter to their family group analyst, who is a staff member, to find out if they really want to see me. They all must analyze if this is something they really want to do. They have to mentally masturbate over my letter, because Harold's bitch-wife says I'm a difficult reality to cope with.

GOLDBERG: Don't you think Harold has a right to relate to whomever and whatever he wishes?

JOSHUA: Harold is my brother!

GOLDBERG: Harold also is a person who can accept or reject whatever he chooses.

JOSHUA: It's that jive-time, bourgeoisie Jewish bitch he's married to with her Christmas trees an' her amputated nose. I asked that bitch what she was doin' sending out Christmas cards an' she told Harold that I was hostile.

GOLDBERG: Was it any concern of yours?

JOSHUA: That bitch don't even know what Chanuka is. Told me she wasn't Jewish 'cause she didn't believe in religion. An' there she was decorating a Christmas tree. I told that chick if the Gestapo knocked on her door, they wouldn't be askin' her if she believed in religion. Man, that chick sure blew her cool behind what I laid on her. She's the one that made him take his number out of the book.

GOLDBERG: A lot of people take their telephone numbers out of the book.

JOSHUA: Harold is my brother an' he should be available to me.

GOLDBERG: Why?

JOSHUA: Because he's my brother!

GOLDBERG: And what does that mean?

JOSHUA: It means that he and I got a slice of the same memory. That's what a man is—his memory. An' me and him got a thousand memories together.

GOLDBERG: You have a strange notion about how people should interrelate.

JOSHUA: That's what Harold use to say to me. Joshua, you gotta learn how to interrelate.

GOLDBERG: He was givin' you sound advice.

JOSHUA: But he didn't want me to interrelate to him.

GOLDBERG: That's his privilege. Now, Joshua, there are one or two questions that I want to ask you.

JOSHUA: Yeah?

GOLDBERG: What is meant by the words: "A rolling stone gathers no moss"?

JOSHUA: [*Rising*] Pardon?

GOLDBERG: "A rolling stone gathers no moss." What do those words imply to you?

JOSHUA: Nothin'.

GOLDBERG: Those words have no meaning to you?

JOSHUA: [*Looking out of bar door*] A tree standing still has a whole heap of moss. Now, what the hell does that mean?

GOLDBERG: "Too many hands in the pot spoils the broth." Now, what does that mean?

JOSHUA: Man, you'd better wake up and see, you might wanna pee. [*Laughs*] Why is it so dark in here? Say, man, I thought hospital s'pose to have white walls.

GOLDBERG: We have white walls.

JOSHUA: Where are they?

GOLDBERG: Beyond that corridor there is another corridor and the walls of that corridor are painted white.

JOSHUA: Le' me see 'em? Let me dig them white walls.

GOLDBERG: [*Opens folder*] Not just yet. There are one or two questions I want to ask you first.

JOSHUA: Never mind the questions. I want to dig them white walls. If the walls are painted white on the other side of the corridor, why ain't they painted white on this side of the corridor?

GOLDBERG: Why is the fact that the walls aren't painted white disturbing you so much?

JOSHUA: 'Cause ev'ry hospital I ever seen had white walls. White walls with big white bulbs hangin' down from white ceilings. An' doctors and nurses dressed in white uniforms, with white shoes and white socks an' white shoelaces. Man, even, like the bed frames are painted white—even the mattresses are white. Serving food out of white plates. Even the disinfectant smells white. Now when I's up in a room with dark, dingy walls an' it smells like ole stale pee an' with dim yellow bulbs hanging from dirty ceilings an' I'm tied up an' wrapped in a red jacket an' bein' told I'm in a hospital by someone I don't know, who is not wearin' white clothes when ev'ryone is suppose to be wearing white clothes, then I want to dig them white walls. You must think I ain't never been in a hospital before. You ain't dealin' with no semi-fool, y'know. You may be pretty foxy, but I done dug you, my man. Peeped your hole card right from the get-go. So you may as well c'mon outta your act.

GOLDBERG: My act?

JOSHUA: Aw, daddy, dig yourself.

GOLDBERG: Just who did you think I am?

JOSHUA: Baby, you know who you are?

GOLDBERG: You tell me.

JOSHUA: I'll tell you who you wanna be.

GOLDBERG: And who do I want to be?

JOSHUA: Th' man!

GOLDBERG: The man?

JOSHUA: Th' man! Th' Boss! Captain Charley himself. Miss Anne's daddy. Th' owner of the big house. Th' one that's got ev'rythin' locked up tight. Master of ev'rythin' he surveys on land an' sea—even much in th' stratosphere. Dr. Yakoo himself. Who took the quiet, peaceful universe an' put it in his pocket. Who harnessed the elements with my backbone. Th' fuzz that's got me tied an' packaged in th' cellar of th' slam. Who asks me questions 'bout trees an' broth an' wants me to give him th' answer that he already knows. But done pulled th' covers offa you, my man. I done open th' closet door an' dug you lurkin' in th' shadows. Minute I open my eyes an' dug you peepin' at me through them bifocals with that Mickey Mouse grin an' that Madison Avenue haircut, I dug what was happenin'.

GOLDBERG: Now, I'm going to ask you some questions about yourself. If there are any questions you don't understand, let me know and I'll repeat the question. Is there anything you want to ask me?

JOSHUA: Yeah. When do I get out of here?

GOLDBERG: I want you to answer the questions as well as you can.

JOSHUA: When do I split the scene?

GOLDBERG: Take a moment and get yourself together.

JOSHUA: I don't have to get myself together, I ain't separated. Like, man, there was a time when I was separated from myself, but I dry-cleaned my brain and got straight.

GOLDBERG: What's your name?

JOSHUA: You know my name, chief.

GOLDBERG: I want you to tell me.

JOSHUA: Look on th' folder.

GOLDBERG: [*Turns folder around*] What's your name?

JOSHUA: Baby, you know my name as well as I do. I mean, like baby, if you don't know what my name is an' you been sittin' up here callin' me by my name—an' you got a folder with my name on it in your hand an' you don't know what my name is, then, like, baby, you belong wrapped up in this thing instead of me.

GOLDBERG: [*Losing his temper*] You're something of a smart aleck, aren't you? Well, I haven't got time for smart alecks. You want to be a wise guy, I can be a wise guy too. Now, either you cooperate with me or I'll have the nurse give you an injection. And when you wake up, if you're still a wise guy, we can give you another injection. Make up your mind! Makes no difference to me one way or the other. If you don't want to answer my questions . . . You know you're only hurting yourself with this hostility. And I'm getting just a little tired of repeating questions over and over again. Listening to you spew out this verbiage in an attempt to avoid answering the simplest question. We have many patients in this ward and I don't have the time to stand here and play games with you. Now, what's it going to be? Medication or cooperation?

JOSHUA: Well, I'll tell you, baby—let you in on a little secret. I dunno my name. I can tell you th' name they call me by, but that ain't really my name. I mean it ain't my real real name. I mean people give you all kinds of names, hateful names, disgustin' names. Names that ain't got nothin' to do with who you are. But after a while if they keep callin' you them names, you get so you start answerin' to them names. Even though you know deep down inside of yourself that them ain't your name. But then pretty soon you get t' think it is your name. An' you are what people are callin' you—mean, ugly, disgusting names. Now that's when you get separated from yourself. An' th' only way to put yourself back together again is to find out where your real name is hidden. 'Cause all the time your real name is hidden someplace just waitin' for you to come and find it. Dig what I mean, chief?

GOLDBERG: I'm going to ask you just one more time for your name.

JOSHUA: That's what I'm tryin' to tell you. I been tagged with a name that ain't my name!

GOLDBERG: What name is that?

JOSHUA: That's th' one you been callin' me by. One you should be tryin' to help me find is th' one that's been hidden from me.

GOLDBERG: You're going to succeed in making me lose my temper. I advise you to try and avoid that.

JOSHUA: Man, like, fuck you and your temper. Why should I lay up here an' listen to this bull- shit? Call up an' get my clothes.

GOLDBERG: I'm not ready to release you.

JOSHUA: Man, you'd better bring me my clothes. Y'can't hold me here against my will. An' I sure hope for your sake nothin' have happen to my clothes. 'Cause they're very expensive clothes an' I'll sue this hospital for ev'ry nickel it's got.

GOLDBERG: [*Checking folder*] Nothing has happened to them. They're downstairs in the admit- ting room with your name on them. Pair of tennis shoes, blue jeans, T-shirt . . . knife.

JOSHUA: What's that?

GOLDBERG: The clothes you were admitted here wear- ing.

JOSHUA: Man, you must have your people mixed up. Baby, that sounds like the wardrobe of a lightweight.

GOLDBERG: That's what you checked in here wearing. It's all down here in the folder.

JOSHUA: Damn that folder. Do I look like a lightweight to you? Do I look like somebody who'd be runnin' 'round in blue jeans an' tennis shoes? Huh? No wonder you been soundin' me down th' way you have. Not givin' me th' respect that I'm due. Callin' me Joshua, a name that ain't my name, but a name that was tagged on me. First my name, now my clothes.

GOLDBERG: Suppose you tell me what you were wearing when you entered the hospital.

JOSHUA: A bright olive-green tunic with dark red print on checkerboard squares, a pair of canary slacks made of the finest Egyptian cotton, gathered at the waist like a short overshirt. A long, loose turquoise robe made of the skin of a lion. A scarlet beret. Oh, yeah—a spear.

GOLDBERG: [*Checking folder*] A switchblade knife.

JOSHUA: When I say "spear," I mean "spear."

GOLDBERG: Why do you carry a knife?

JOSHUA: A spear! Only shortstops carry switchblade knives, baby! A spear! A long leaf or slender stalk consisting of a pointed head of a long shift. A weapon with a sharp head or blade for thrusting or throwing. A similar barbed instrument for catching fish. I know the difference between a knife and a spear. So don't be tryin' to pawn no switchblade knife on me.

GOLDBERG: I think you better get back into the bed.

JOSHUA: I had enough of that bed.

GOLDBERG: Are you going to get back into that bed?

JOSHUA: Are you going to get me my clothes?

GOLDBERG: Do you want me to call the attendant and have him put you back in the bed?

JOSHUA: Aw, man, you're really somethin'.

GOLDBERG: Just relax. [*Pushes him gently back onto bed*]

JOSHUA: I ain't tense.

GOLDBERG: Do you have any idea why you're here, Joshua?

JOSHUA: Don't you know?

GOLDBERG: You tell me.

JOSHUA: If you don't know, you don't have any right to hold me here.

GOLDBERG: Is it that you don't remember what you did?

JOSHUA: Naw, s'pose you run it down to me.

GOLDBERG: You don't remember going to an office building and exposing yourself indecently to an office full of women? You have no recollection of that act?

JOSHUA: I don't know what you mean.

GOLDBERG: You don't know what "indecent exposure" means?

JOSHUA: Naw, what does it mean?

GOLDBERG: You know very well what it means. You committed an act of hostility against and directed at a number of young ladies in a midtown office building.

JOSHUA: Y'mean 'cause I took a piss?

GOLDBERG: You urinated on their floor!

JOSHUA: I had to take a pee.

GOLDBERG: You exposed a room full of women . . .

JOSHUA: I'm circumcised.

GOLDBERG: [*Ignoring his last remark*] Does that seem like rational behavior to you?

JOSHUA: Kidneys ain't rational. I asked that little sweet-water faggot to let me use the john and he wouldn't do it.

GOLDBERG: So you urinated on their floor.

JOSHUA: When you gotta go you gotta go.

GOLDBERG: That speaks well for your race.

JOSHUA: What?

GOLDBERG: I'm sorry, I didn't mean that. [*Slight pause*] How did you come to be in the office?

JOSHUA: [*After a pause*] I was lookin' for a job.

GOLDBERG: Will you please tell me how you thought you could get a job by exposing yourself and using their floor as a toilet? Had anything happened to you before you arrived at the office?

JOSHUA: Me an' th' starter got into a rumble.

GOLDBERG: The starter? What occurred between you and him?

JOSHUA: I didn't want to ride the elevator.

GOLDBERG: You didn't want to ride the elevator where?

JOSHUA: Fiftieth floor.

GOLDBERG: Well . . . how were you going to get up there—to the fiftieth floor?

JOSHUA: Walk?

GOLDBERG: You were going to walk up fifty flights of stairs?

JOSHUA: I don't like elevators.

GOLDBERG: Are you afraid to ride in elevators?

JOSHUA: I just don't like ridin' in 'em.

GOLDBERG: Why do you think they install elevators? Obviously they can't have people walking up and down fifty flights of stairs, now, can they? Wouldn't it have been simpler to just get into the elevator and ride up the fifty flights of stairs instead of becoming upset over a trifle? I mean they have set up certain procedures which are used in the transporting of people through the building. And they have the right to set up what they consider to be the most efficient system of getting people up to and down from the various floors, correct?

JOSHUA: Then what did they put the staircase in for? Huh? Dig it, chief? They got fifty flights of stairs which they keep under lock and key. An' they, like, man, blow their stack if somebody wants to walk on their precious staircase.

GOLDBERG: Why do you suppose a building has a staircase that is closed to the general public? Could it be in case of fire?

JOSHUA: But they keep all the doors locked on every floor. I checked every door all the way up to the fiftieth floor.

GOLDBERG: Why do you think they don't allow people to walk on their staircase?

JOSHUA: That's what I was tryin' t' find out from

the lame who was th' starter. An', chief, you should have dug that chump. He looked like one of them South American dictators, dressed in a white uniform with a black hat and gloves and sunglasses.

GOLDBERG: How did you get up to the office?

JOSHUA: I walked up.

GOLDBERG: The starter let you walk up?

JOSHUA: Naw, after I sounded that lame down an' told him I'd put somethin' on his ass, he went runnin' after a cop. So I picked the lock with my spear an' walked up th' stairs.

GOLDBERG: You walked up fifty flights of stairs rather than take the elevator? Does that seem like normal behavior to you?

JOSHUA: I don't know what you mean, daddy.

GOLDBERG: Never mind. Just go on.

JOSHUA: So I falls into th' office, y'understand? An', man, what I spied almost made me flip my lid right there on th' spot. I couldn't quite bring it into focus all at once but as I dug th' scene more closely—like, man, it hit me.

GOLDBERG: What hit you?

JOSHUA: Noses!

GOLDBERG: Noses?

JOSHUA: Like, man, there musta been a hundred chicks in that place, y'dig? An', man, they were all divided by noses. Yeah. I mean, like, all th' chicks on th' left side of the room had Jewish noses an' all th' chicks on th' right side of the room had Christian noses. An' amongst the Christian noses I spied some castrated noses.

GOLDBERG: What's this obsession you have about other people's noses?

JOSHUA: They were all separated and divided from each other by their noses. Man, the separatin' of them noses almost unwrapped my hatband. So I just stood there tryin' to figure out exactly what was th' main idea of this setup. An' b'fore I could work out

THUNDER IN THE INDEX | 103

this whole thin', down th' aisle came this little sweet-water faggot. An' y' know what this little faggot asked me: "May I help you?" So I cut into this faggot an' ask him exactly what it was he wanted to help me do. Like, I don't care 'bout th' way a cat gets his kicks.

GOLDBERG: Are you hostile against homosexuals?

JOSHUA: Man, I ain't hostile against nobody. I just don't dig cats who are turned around.

GOLDBERG: Do they threaten you in some way?

JOSHUA: Man, I wished one of them lames would come up threatenin' me. Man, I'd take care of business so quick he wouldn't know what was happenin', I'd go upside his knot.

GOLDBERG: I didn't mean any kind of physical threat.

JOSHUA: What kind of threat do you mean?

GOLDBERG: I don't know. I'm trying to find out from you.

JOSHUA: What is it you're tryin' t' find out, my man?

GOLDBERG: You have any particular animosity against someone who you might feel is homosexual?

JOSHUA: Man, I ain't puttin' fags down. Like, if you think I am . . . Like, if I've stepped on your toes . . .

GOLDBERG: Stepped on my toes? How's that? What do you mean?

JOSHUA: Like, I don't care 'bout th' way a cat gets his kicks. Like, dig, if you're dealin' in th' closet, an' I ain't sayin' that you are . . .

GOLDBERG: Just what are you implying?

JOSHUA: I ain't implyin' nothin', my man.

GOLDBERG: You seem to be implying something—now, what is it?

JOSHUA: Nothin'.

GOLDBERG: What are you suggesting?

JOSHUA: Man, I ain't worryin' about who is an' who ain't. Like, all I know you could be a closet queen. Whole lotta closet queens, y'know. I mean you look straight, but I ain't followin' you around. I don't know what you do under th' covers when th' lights go out.

GOLDBERG: [*Holding his temper. Changing the subject*] You say you went to the office building to seek employment.

JOSHUA: Yeah.

GOLDBERG: Did you see the person who was doing hiring?

JOSHUA: Naw, th' little faggot handed me an application form. So I sounded th' cat down. I mean, I wanted to know if th' position was still open. Told me I'd haffta fill out th' application form b'fore he could tell me if th' gig was still open or not. Well, I tried to run it down on th' clown that I don't dig fillin' out application forms. Man, th' cat started breakin' out into a cold sweat. Got mad 'cause I didn't want to fill out his application form.

GOLDBERG: Do you object to filling out application forms?

JOSHUA: Them things make me wanna almost blow my stack.

GOLDBERG: Why do they bother you? Do you know?

JOSHUA: 'Cause them things make me almost wanna blow my stack.

GOLDBERG: You get upset over application forms?

JOSHUA: Yeah.

GOLDBERG: Why do they bother you?

JOSHUA: Because I am supposed to set down in chronological order the history of Joshua Noon on a pink card seven and one half inches by seven and one half inches. In spaces designed in little boxes, which were not scaled for who Joshua Noon is. To break up the history of Joshua Noon an' then fit it into them tiny little boxes. Man, I can't be broken down like that an' made to fit into them little boxes. Man, ain't noway in th' world nobody can tell who I am by readin' little pieces of me outta little boxes that ain't even made to scale. Like, there ain't enough space on a thousand and one of them things to tell who I am. So when that little faggot handed me that application form I was really shook up, like, uptight. Have you ever dug one of them application forms, my man? Question number 1: Where did you hear about us? Question number 2: What is your regular occupation? Question number 3: What kind of position do you want with us? Question number 4: A: Work experience; list your last job first. B: Name and address of firm. C: Employed from month, day and year. In a space three quarters of an inch long I'm supposed to put down the day—the exact day, month, an' year I started to work, plus the salary I made per hour and per week. An' in another box half that size I have to write down the exact day, month, an' year I quit, plus my reason for quitting, plus my immediate supervisor; plus the title of the work I did, plus a description of the work I did, plus the kind of work supervised by me. You have to make out seven of them damn last-job-first sections. Question number 5: Do you have any disability? Yes or no? Describe. So you know what I describe? My opinion of the goddamn application forms. Question number 6: Who should we call in case of emergency? Now, what kind of a fool question is that? Who would you call but a doctor? Question number 7: Professional, trade or scientific organizations to which you belong. Now, what the hell would anyone be doin' in this zoo if he had a trade or profession! Question number 8: Thesis, professional or trade papers—give title, date and if published, where? D'y' know what I put down? The left wall of the men's room on th' I.R.T. subway station at Times Square. Question number 9: Current licenses or certificates—teaching, engineering, etc. by state or city. Question number 10: Will commute: Yes or no? If yes, where? Now, how should I know where this place will want me to commute! Will relocate (b) Yes or no? If yes, where? (c) Will travel? Yes or no? If yes, where? Question 11: Do you drive a car? Yes or no? (b) Is car available for use? Yes or no? Question 12: Box: The New York Law against discrimination prohibits discrimination because of age, race or sex. Question 13: Education: Grade school: name and location of grade school. High school: name and location. Day slash month slash year. No goddamn place to answer. College? Major? Minor? Other credits. Professional or technical school? List foreign languages below. Speak: Excellent? Good? Fair? Read: Excellent? Good? Fair? Write: Excellent? Good? Fair? Signature. You may check my references with the above mentioned firms. Now why in the hell do I have to answer all of that to apply for a job cleaning shit bowls in the Executive Washroom?

GOLDBERG: Did you want the job?

JOSHUA: I needed the job. An' not once—not no place on that goddamn card did they ask me if I wanted or needed a job. They did not ask me if my room had to be paid for or if my stomach had to be filled.

GOLDBERG: Filling out the application form was part of the procedure to acquire the position, was it not?

JOSHUA: Now, why do I have to know a foreign language to be the porter of the Executive Washroom? Do they fart in French?

GOLDBERG: You didn't have to fill out the application form. You could have walked right out of the office.

JOSHUA: Like I told you, I needed the job.

GOLDBERG:	Filling out the application was one of the steps necessary, wasn't it?
JOSHUA:	I filled out th' damn thing an' he still didn't give me th' job.
GOLDBERG:	Well, not that he had to, but did he give you any reason?
JOSHUA:	No, he just took my application and said he would keep it on file. So I told th' fag to give me my application back an' I'd leave my telephone number. Said he couldn't give it back to me. It was th' policy of th' company to keep application forms on file.
GOLDBERG:	Well, it was company property.
JOSHUA:	It belonged to me.
GOLDBERG:	How did it belong to you? It wasn't paid for by you, was it?
JOSHUA:	It had my whole life history on it—from th' month, day an' year I was born.
GOLDBERG:	But it still was not your property. It was the private property of the company. Do you think you have the right to seize other people's private property? Now, no one forced you or sent you to that office. You came there of your own free will and volition, supposedly seeking employment. They have a right to set up those methods and procedures which they feel necessary for the handling of employment in the most efficient manner possible.
JOSHUA:	All I wanted was my application form back.
GOLDBERG:	Your application form. How is it yours? Did you buy the paper? Did you pay for the cost of the printing? Did you design the series of questions that appeared on the form?
JOSHUA:	What the hell did they need it for?
GOLDBERG:	Analysis! Those answers had to be weighed and balanced so that a total image of your personality emerged.
JOSHUA:	My image is my personal property.
GOLDBERG:	Did anyone force you to fill out the form?

JOSHUA: That little faggot! An' he wouldn't give it back to me.

GOLDBERG: Why didn't you leave?

JOSHUA: I wanted back my form with the contents of my whole existence.

GOLDBERG: But it was no longer your property.

JOSHUA: Man, like, that cat had taken my soul and filed it away in one of them steel drawers!

GOLDBERG: He was following company policy.

JOSHUA: Was it their policy not to let me go to the bathroom? I ask that little faggot where the men's room was and he ignored me.

GOLDBERG: You couldn't control yourself until you found a place that would accept you?

JOSHUA: I found a place. Right in the middle of their floor.

NURSE: [*At door with tray*] Doctor? [*She enters.*]

GOLDBERG: [*Moves down toward her*] Did you locate 2A?

NURSE: We've searched the floor over and over again. He must have slipped out. The only thing to do is call the police and give them a description.

GOLDBERG: [*Inspecting tray*] What's this?

NURSE: Blood test.

GOLDBERG: Blood test?

NURSE: Routine. We generally check for traces of narcotics.

GOLDBERG: [*Moving back to* JOSHUA] Are you on drugs, Joshua?

JOSHUA: Is your mother on drugs?

GOLDBERG: We're going to take a sample of your blood.

JOSHUA: My blood's red, I can tell you that.

GOLDBERG: I'm sure it is. All we want to know is whether or not there is any trace of narcotics in the bloodstream.

JOSHUA: Suppose I say no?

NURSE: The court gives us the legal right to take a blood sample.

JOSHUA: Th' court? How you sound? I don't give you no right. How's th' court gonna give you the right to stick me with a needle.

THUNDER IN THE INDEX | 109

	Like, what kinda hype you tryin' to run down on me, my man? Now, th' court's gonna give you th' right to cop th' blood outta me regardless of how I feel about it.
NURSE:	[*Preparing the needle*] That's correct.
JOSHUA:	Chick, you ain't correct. Don't you know this here is America—land of th' free an' th' home of th' brave? An' every man's house is his castle. Well, my body is my castle. An' I don't give you permission to invade my castle with no long-pointed needles.
NURSE:	[*Pouring alcohol on cotton*] Now, no one's going to hurt you, Joshua.
JOSHUA:	I know damn well you ain't 'cause you ain't gonna stick me with no needle.
NURSE:	Should I call for help, Doctor?
GOLDBERG:	Help?
JOSHUA:	You can call for Jesus Christ if you want to. But you still ain't stickin' me with no needle.
NURSE:	Should I call for an attendant?
GOLDBERG:	You take the sample. I'll hold him down.
JOSHUA:	Take this thing offa me an' we'll see how you hold me down.
NURSE:	Now, Joshua, we're all your friends here.
JOSHUA:	Get away from me. You ain't takin' my blood.
NURSE:	Now, Doctor . . . [GOLDBERG *leaps on him and drags him, struggling, to bed. The* NURSE *ties a piece of rubber around his arm, rubs it with alcohol.*] The vein isn't very good in this arm. Open and close your hand.
JOSHUA:	Go to hell.
GOLDBERG:	Try the other arm.
NURSE:	Maybe I can get enough out of this one. Now just try and relax. [*He screams as she plunges needle into his arm.*] Don't be such a baby! I'm not hurting you that much.
JOSHUA:	Don't bleed me!
GOLDBERG:	Just relax and keep still.

NURSE:	He'd better keep still if he doesn't want this needle broken off in his arm.
JOSHUA:	You put it over on 'em, didn't you, my man?
GOLDBERG:	Put what over?
JOSHUA:	Y'know where it's at, chief.
GOLDBERG:	What are you talking about?
JOSHUA:	You done laid it on 'em. How did you do it, chief?
GOLDBERG:	Do what?
JOSHUA:	You know what. How did you get out, chief? How did you get outta this thing—an' outta th' room?
NURSE:	What's he talking about?
GOLDBERG:	I have no idea.
JOSHUA:	Man, you know where I'm at. Just like I know where you're at.
GOLDBERG:	Open your mouth once more and I'll have you put under sedation.
JOSHUA:	Ouch!
NURSE:	Think someone was trying to murder you.
JOSHUA:	It hurts.
NURSE:	It's only alcohol. [*Rubbing his arm with alcohol*]
JOSHUA:	It's cold.
NURSE:	I'll run a test on it.
JOSHUA:	You done got free now so you're gonna steal th' blood outta my arm.
GOLDBERG:	You better lie down.
JOSHUA:	I done dug you, my man. Slipped outta this thing an' got outta th' room.
GOLDBERG:	I think you'd better lie down, Joshua.
JOSHUA:	You may be foxy enough to pull th' wool over ev'rybody's eyes, but I done dug you, my man. I see right through your act. Came in here tryin' to exercise your game on me.
NURSE:	Doctor?
JOSHUA:	He ain't no doctor! I'm gonna scream on you, my man.
GOLDBERG:	You'd better get that test up to the lab.
JOSHUA:	[*Moving to chair and begins shaking*] Yes, go on, Nurse.
NURSE:	What's he doing?

GOLDBERG: I don't know.
NURSE: It's not that cold in here.
GOLDBERG: Get back in bed, Joshua.
JOSHUA: Not until I finished.
GOLDBERG: Finished what?
JOSHUA: You know what.
GOLDBERG: I want you back in the bed.
JOSHUA: Soon as I finished sittin' shiver for you, my man.
GOLDBERG: Sitting shiver!
NURSE: What does he mean?
GOLDBERG: Nothing. Did you hear me tell you to take that blood up to the lab? Don't just stand there.
NURSE: I think I should call for one of the attendants.
GOLDBERG: I don't need an attendant!
NURSE: Doctor . . .
GOLDBERG: I want you out of that chair and into the bed. Do you hear me, Joshua? Get into the bed.
JOSHUA: Are there any songs that go with sitting shiver, my man?
GOLDBERG: Damn you, you black bastard!
JOSHUA: Thought that wasn't your word, chief.
GOLDBERG: Nurse! Medication! Medication!

[NURSE *exits with tray.*]

JOSHUA: Take this damn thing offa me.
GOLDBERG: Don't worry, you won't feel it shortly.
JOSHUA: You're gonna knock me out, huh? That what you gonna do, Cousin Goldberg?
GOLDBERG: [*At bars*] Nurse! Hurry with that medication!
JOSHUA: You're gonna turn off my lights, huh?
GOLDBERG: I've had all I'm going to take off of you. You are going to sit shiver for me. Huh? Well, we'll see. I should have done this the first time you started heaping your abuses on me.

JOSHUA: You ain't no doctor. You're nothing but another patient like me. Don't you know that, you clown?

GOLDBERG: Hurry with that medication.

JOSHUA: They're going to find your ass out an' then I hope you'll be back in that room tied up in one of these things.

NURSE: [*Enters with needle*] Here it is, Doctor.

GOLDBERG: Can you administer it?

NURSE: Yes, Doctor. [*She moves toward* JOSHUA *with the needle.*]

JOSHUA: I'll wake up. You can't keep knocking me out.

GOLDBERG: When you wake up and don't behave yourself, then you'll get another one.

NURSE: Stand still, Joshua.

JOSHUA: Get away from me, devil. You're the devil. The blue-eyed devil!

NURSE: Now, Joshua . . . [*She plunges the needle into his ass.*]

JOSHUA: You went and did it, didn't you? [*Dazed, he moves toward the bed.*] You done gone an' put my lights out. [*Falls onto bed*]

NURSE: [*Trying to straighten him on bed*] Doctor, could you give me a hand, please?

GOLDBERG: Of course.

NURSE: I just can't understand how 2A was able to slip out of here. We've never had anyone escape from here before.

GOLDBERG: No.

NURSE: Oh, occasionally a patient gets out of his room. But never off the floor.

GOLDBERG: Perhaps we'd better have a review of security measures.

NURSE: We have such a changing staff all the time —security is hard to maintain.

GOLDBERG: [*Pause*] I hated to do that.

NURSE: I beg your pardon?

GOLDBERG: I don't like to use such measures with a patient.

NURSE: You had no choice.

GOLDBERG: Yes.

NURSE: These nig—people are hard to deal with.

GOLDBERG: Nurse?

NURSE: Yes?

GOLDBERG: Did you ever hear that Jews are niggers turned inside out?

NURSE: I beg your pardon?

GOLDBERG: I said did you ever hear that Jews are niggers turned inside out?

NURSE: I'm afraid I don't know what you mean.

GOLDBERG: Do you consider that Jews and niggers are first cousins?

NURSE: Doctor, are you all right?

GOLDBERG: Of course, I'm all right. I asked you a question, Nurse.

NURSE: Doctor, I don't know what you're talking about.

GOLDBERG: You know damn well what I'm talking about. What right did you have to think I was Irish or Italian?

NURSE: Doctor, I think I'd better take the tray back.

GOLDBERG: [Blocking door] You didn't answer me.

NURSE: I don't really know what you are trying to find out.

GOLDBERG: You know all right.

NURSE: Doctor, please, let me by.

GOLDBERG: Where do you have to go?

NURSE: I'm the only registered nurse on this floor.

GOLDBERG: I see. [Moves away from door] All right, you may go. [NURSE exits with tray. GOLDBERG moves to foot of bed and looks down on the sleeping form of JOSHUA.] Joshua Noon?

[The sound of a flute is heard somewhere way off in the distance of his mind. He shakes his head and the music fades. He moves to table and pours himself a glass of water.]

NURSE:	[*Enters*] How are you feeling, Doctor?
GOLDBERG:	That music . . .
NURSE:	What kind of music, Doctor?
GOLDBERG:	Just music . . .
NURSE:	Flute music?
GOLDBERG:	What makes you think I heard flute music?
NURSE:	I love flute music.
GOLDBERG:	You do?
NURSE:	Would you come with me, Doctor?
GOLDBERG:	Come with you? Come with you where?
NURSE:	Back to 2A.
GOLDBERG:	Back to 2A! What do you mean?
NURSE:	You know what I mean, don't you, Doctor?
GOLDBERG:	Nurse, have you lost your mind?
NURSE:	Now, c'mon quietly, Doctor.
GOLDBERG:	If you don't get the hell out of here.
NURSE:	[*Through the bars*] All right, boys—come get him.

[*Two blonde husky* ATTENDANTS *rush in. One carries a straitjacket.*]

GOLDBERG:	What's the meaning of this? Nurse, are you out of your mind?
NURSE:	There is no way to get off this floor.
GOLDBERG:	Get them out of here.
FIRST ATTENDANT:	Now come peacefully, Doctor. We don't want to hurt you.
SECOND ATTENDANT:	[*Showing him a straitjacket*] Look what we've brought for you.
GOLDBERG:	You're not going to put that thing on me.
FIRST ATTENDANT:	Don't make us have to get rough.
NURSE:	Doctor.
GOLDBERG:	[*Backing into corner*] Now, just one minute . . . [FIRST ATTENDANT *leaps upon him and brings him to floor. The* SECOND ATTENDANT *forces his arms into jacket.*] You can't do this to me. I'm Doctor Samuel Goldberg. A resident staff member of this institution. You can't do this to me. Do you know who I am?

THUNDER IN THE INDEX | 115

SECOND ATTENDANT: Yes, we know who you are.
FIRST ATTENDANT: A staff member of this institution.
GOLDBERG: Help! Help!! Help!!!

[*The* NURSE *reveals a needle in her hand.
She moves toward the* DOCTOR *and plunges
it into him. After a moment he faints. The*
TWO ATTENDANTS *pick him up and carry
him out, followed by the* NURSE. *The lights
dim slowly on the sleeping form of* JOSHUA
in the bed.]

THIS BIRD OF DAWNING
SINGETH ALL NIGHT LONG

● ● ● ● ● ● ● ● ●

"Some say that ever gainst that season comes
Wherein our Saviour's birth is celebrated
This Bird of Dawning Singeth all Night Long"

A one-room efficiency apartment in a recently constructed building on New York's renewed Upper East Side. The room has been designed in the shape of the letter L. The entrance is a metal door cut into the back wall. The left and right walls are separated by about eighteen feet. The left wall runs about half the length of the right and houses an open kitchen up stage left. It curves and creates another back wall with a metal door which is the entrance to the bathroom. A far-left wall creates the space for the bedroom. A modern replica of the old-fashioned brass bed has been mounted on a platform, raised about a half foot off the floor. A Tiffany lamp hangs down over the bed. Next to the bed is a table with lines of colored bottles with various colored pills and liquid medicines.

The right wall runs straight down into the audience. Placed against the wall running in an almost straight line is a couch, a hi-fi set, and a dinette set with a matching whiskey cabinet.

The curtain rises on the dark apartment around three or four o'clock in the morning. We hear the sound of ANNE JILLETT *having a nightmare. Suddenly out of the dark silence we hear the sound of a telephone ringing. She rises up in her bed, frightened. She is a woman in her midthirties with a face in the first stages of decay. She waits for a moment, hoping the phone will cease to ring. Finally she rises, crosses to the dinette area and lifts the white telephone on top of the whiskey cabinet.*

ANNE: Hello, who is it? Nancy? Nancy who? Ferrett? I don't know anyone by that name. Yes, this is Anne Jillett, but I don't know anyone named Nancy Ferrett. How did you get my number? What? I don't think it's any concern of yours why I'm not listed in the book. Is this someone's idea of a sense of humor, because I don't think it's funny. I'm afraid you must have made some kind of mistake. Goodbye. [*She hangs up the phone, snaps off the light and returns to bed. The phone rings again, this time louder and even more intense! She leaps out of bed to stop the frightening sound.*] Hello! Yes, this is Anne Jillett. Oh, it's you again. Didn't I tell you I don't know you? Will you please stop calling me? I don't know you. Don't you understand that? I don't care what your name is. Now, just stop calling me at two o'clock in the morning, will you please? I did not tell you to call me and I most assuredly didn't give you my number. Where did you get it? Stop it! Stoppitt! I didn't give you my telephone number and stop saying that I did. . . . I don't want to talk to you about anything. I did not tell you that I had anything to discuss with you. I don't even know you. Maybe you have the wrong Anne Jillett. What? What do you mean? I don't know what you mean. Now, look, I don't know who put you up to this, but you better stop calling me before I call the police. I'll call the cops and have you arrested, is that perfectly clear? They can trace the call and find the place you're calling from. I'm not lying! They have a little thing they can put on the phone and some way they have of finding out where the call is coming from. I don't know what they call it. I read about it . . . I don't remember where . . . None of your goddamn business where I read about it. Don't call me a liar! I don't have to tell you where I read about it. Stop it! Stop it! Do you hear me? I'm not a liar! Are you some kind of lunatic? I don't have to put up with this. [*Hangs up the phone*] People they let run around loose in the city, it's a crying shame. [*She crosses to the liquor cabinet and pours herself a drink. She moves to the bedroom and takes a pill and washes it down with liquor. She turns out the light and immediately the phone starts ringing again. She runs to the phone and removes it from the hook, clicks several times to break the connection. She takes it off the hook, but it continues to ring. She pulls the plug out of the wall and snatches the receiver, but still it continues to ring. Slowly she begins to recognize that it is the doorbell and not the phone. She runs to the door.*] Who is it?

NANCY: Is dat yuh, Miss Anne, honey?

ANNE: Who is it? Who's out there?

NANCY: [*From other side of door*] It's me, Miss Anne, honey.
           Nancy . . . Ferrett.

ANNE: Get away. Get away from here.

NANCY: Ain't youh gwine open up dis do'r n' let me in, sugar?

ANNE: You better get away from here before I call the police.

NANCY: Is you is or is you ain't gwine open up this heah do'?

ANNE: [*Panic-stricken*] Will you please go away and leave
           me alone? [*She runs to the broken telephone and tries
           to get the operator.*] Operator! Operator! [*Realizing
           phone is broken, she becomes hysterical. She runs to
           window and tries to raise it and discovers it's stuck.
           She tries to holler through the window.*] Help! You
           down there, look up here! Please, look up here!

           [*The door to the apartment swings open and* NANCY
           FERRETT *enters. She is a black-skinned woman about
           the same size and age of* ANNE, *dressed in a heavy
           worn coat, a pair of dirty white tennis shoes, with a
           red bandana tied around her head. She carries two
           shopping bags full of junk.*]

NANCY: [*Adjusting to the darkness*] Miss Anne . . . where is
           youh, child? Youh ain't hidin' from me, is youh?

ANNE: You—you get out of here!

NANCY: Oh, dere youh is.

ANNE: [*Trying to get past her*] You get out of here before I
           scream.

NANCY: Scream?

ANNE: I'll wake up the whole building. I'll scream bloody
           murder.

NANCY: Scream bloody murder? Girl, what youh so upset
           about?

ANNE: [*Pushes her*] Get out of here!

NANCY: [*Breaks away, barring door*] What you pushing on me
           for?

ANNE: [*Breaks for door*] Let me out of here!

NANCY: Girl, y' can't go out in your nightclothes! Folks'll think
           you've taken leave of youh senses.

ANNE: [*Screams*] Help!

NANCY: [*Cupping her mouth with her hand*] What youh screamin' 'bout, honey lamb? Girl, does y' wanna wake up der whole house? Folks is trying to sleep. Now I'm gwine let y' go but don't youh be screamin' like that no mo'!

ANNE: What do you want? You want money? [*She finds her purse and takes money, offers it.*] Here, take it.

NANCY: What is youh givin' me yo' money fer? I don't want nona yo' ole money, gal.

ANNE: You don't want to hurt me?

NANCY: I don't go 'round hurtin' folks.

ANNE: Then what are you doing here?

NANCY: Now, youh knows what I'm doin' heah. Sho' can ask some fool questions.

ANNE: Who are you?

NANCY: Who is I? Now you know who I is.

ANNE: No . . .?

NANCY: Youh know good 'n' well who I is.

ANNE: No, I don't.

NANCY: Now, why does youh wanna play like youh don't know who I is?

ANNE: I tell you I don't know you.

NANCY: Lawd, der child wants t' play like she don't know who in der world I is. Sho' didn't think you'd ever do me like dis. No sir, Jesus. If somebody had told me, I sho wouldn'da believed dem.

ANNE: You must have me mixed up with someone else. That's it. It's all just a question of mistaken identity.

NANCY: Sho' is a big word. I ain't all together sho' I understands that word.

ANNE: Maybe I look like someone you used to know. Now, think . . . [*She tries to move past her toward the door.*] Think about it for a minute. Must be someone who I look a little like.

NANCY: Yo' name is Anne Jillett, ain't it?

ANNE: Maybe she had a name similar to mine.

NANCY: I know youh almost as good as I know myself.

ANNE: [*Leaps to door*] Help!

NANCY: [*Catches her and drags her back into room*] Now where does youh think you're gwine?

ANNE: [*Falls on couch*] Let go of me, you black . . .

NANCY: Now, why does youh wanna call me names? Sho' wouldn't call youh no names.

ANNE: This is my house. You get out of here.

NANCY: Well, what did youh invite me fer?

ANNE: Invite you?

NANCY: Youh sho' enough did. Sent me dis key . . .

ANNE: Where did you get the key to my apartment?

NANCY: Youh gave it to me, Miss Anne, honey.

ANNE: You're a liar!

NANCY: Youh sent dis key n' told me t' c'mon.

ANNE: You're a dirty black liar!

NANCY: Doncha be callin' me no liar.

ANNE: Where did you get the key? Lenny Redmond? Lenny Redmond sent you here, didn't he?

NANCY: Whose dat? Don't recollect knowin' nobody by dat name.

ANNE: He gave you the key to my apartment and told you where I lived, didn't he? He sent you here and put you up to this, didn't he?

NANCY: I don't know what in de Lawd's name youh is talkin' 'bout, child.

ANNE: Stop lying! I know he sent you here.

NANCY: Den youh sho' know mo' den I does.

ANNE: He knows I have a bad heart, so he sent you here to frighten me. Thought I'd die of a heart attack. After all I did for him, this is how he repays me. I got him out of jail . . . fed him, clothed him. This is how he pays me back. Frightening me to death isn't enough. He has to try and humiliate me by sending something like you here. I'll fix him! I'll fix him good. I want you to come with me to the police. I want you to tell them how he gave you the key to my apartment, told you where I lived, and paid you to come here and terrorize me.

NANCY: Ain't nobody paid me nuthin'.

ANNE: How did he make you do it?

NANCY: Ain't nobody made me do nuthin', I keep telling' you.

ANNE: He's using you.

NANCY: Who's usin' me?

ANNE: Lenny Redmond!

NANCY: Ain't I done told you I don't know nobody by dat

name? Youh sho' is hard t' make understand once youh gets somethin' in yo' mind.

ANNE: You stupid nigger! You don't have enough intelligence to know when you're being used. He probably made you think he was your friend, didn't he? He wouldn't spit on something like you if he couldn't use you. Don't you know that? No, you don't have that many brains. I know it—I know it just as sure as I know my heart is pounding that he sent you here. So stop trying to protect him. You don't have enough common sense to know what he is. Do you know that he's a gangster, a criminal? That he'll lie and cheat and steal? Even try and commit—murder? No, you don't know that, you poor fool. I could almost feel sorry for you. [*She pauses.*] Do you believe in God? Of course you do. Do you know that he doesn't? He laughs at people who do. He makes fun of them—tells jokes about them.

NANCY: He laughs at folks what believes in de Lawd? 'N' he's a friend of yourn? How in de world did youh ever get hooked up wit' some'in' like him?

ANNE: I needed him once. I needed him so badly I just closed my eyes to what he really was.

NANCY: Sho' oughta be ashame of yourself. Never would I get hooked up with folks that don't believes in de Lawd.

ANNE: It was the greatest mistake of my life.

NANCY: Tellin' me it wuz.

ANNE: Come with me.

NANCY: Come wit' youh where?

ANNE: Because I want you to tell them . . .

NANCY: Tell dem what?

ANNE: The truth about Lenny Redmond.

NANCY: Reckon ain't no usta keepin' tellin' youh I don't know nuttin' 'bout him. 'Cause youh is bound a determin' I does.

ANNE: [*Attacks her*] Tell the truth!

NANCY: Is you done gone crazy?

[*They fall to the floor.*]

ANNE: [*Furious*] You're gonna tell the truth or I'm gonna kill you. [*Choking her*]

NANCY: Youh better let go of me!

ANNE: I'll kill you . . . you black bitch!

NANCY: [*Struggling*] I can't breathe!

ANNE: I'm gonna choke your black tongue out! I'm gonna pull it out through your rotten teeth!

NANCY: Don't kill me, Miss Anne! Please, don't kill me, Miss Anne!

ANNE: Beg me not to kill you, nigger! Beg me!

NANCY: I'm begging youh, Miss Anne. I's abeggin'.

ANNE: You'll know better than to come breaking into someone else's apartment, won't you?

NANCY: Yes'm, Miss Anne!

ANNE: Oh, how I hate you, you stinking black bitch!

NANCY: Yes'm, Miss Anne. Yes ma'm, youh sho' is right.

ANNE: I could just kill you and nothing would be done about it. Just another nigger dead.

NANCY: [*Works her hand into pocket, pulls out knife*] Yes'm. [*Eases knife to* ANNE's *throat.*] Git offa me or I'll cut you' gizza out. Just roll on over 'n' play dead.

[ANNE *rolls over off of her.*]

ANNE: I should've killed you.

NANCY: [*Getting to her feet*] Youh sho' tried hard 'nough. Dis der way youh treat all yo' company?

ANNE: [*Still on the floor*] You're not my company.

NANCY: Reckon pretty soon youh'll be sayin' we ain't even much no kin.

ANNE: Kin?

NANCY: Blood kin.

ANNE: You! Kin to me! [*She laughs.*]

NANCY: What you laughin' 'bout, like youh crazy?

ANNE: What kin could I be to something like you?

NANCY: Sho' didn't think youh'd treat me like dis. What'cha invite me here fer if dis wuz de way youh wuz gwine treat me? Sho' didn't think my own sister would do me like dis.

ANNE: Sister?

NANCY: By blood!

ANNE: You crazy fool, when did they let you out?

NANCY: Sho' does hurt when you' own flesh n' blood call y' bad names.

ANNE: I'm not your flesh and blood.

NANCY: Yes, youh is.

ANNE: God in heaven.

NANCY: Wrote me all dem letters. Invitin' me up heah t' cum stay wit' y'. Don't know what's gotten int' y'.

ANNE: What letters?

NANCY: [*Dumps shopping bags*] Heah yo' lies—ev'ryone of 'em.

ANNE: [*Recognizing letters*] Where did you get these?

NANCY: From youh!

ANNE: These are letters I wrote to my sister.

NANCY: Lies youh wrote to me.

ANNE: I wrote these to my sister before she died.

NANCY: Now, how can I be dead 'n' I'm standin' heah big as life?

ANNE: How did you get them?

NANCY: Youh wrote them to me.

ANNE: I wrote them to my twin sister, Nancy.

NANCY: But I is yo' twin sister, Nancy.

ANNE: [*Praying*] Oh, God, please . . . please, dear God help me. Help me before it's too late. Something black and evil is happening to me. Some strange, dark, terrible thing is tormenting me.

NANCY: [*Places hand on her head and prays*] Help my po' sister, sweet Jesus. Touch her heart with your divine hand and purify it.

ANNE: Deliver this evil, black thing from me, God.

NANCY: Help her, oh Lord, t' see th' light that's burnin' in my heart. Help her to be guided by that light.

ANNE: Come down, God, and strike this evil black thing dead.

NANCY: She's one of Yo'r lost lambs, Jesus. In Thine name, Amen.

ANNE: [*Begging*] Let me out of here, please . . .

NANCY: Now, you don't wanna go runnin' 'round through these cold, drafty hallways, d'ya? You sure looks tire—why don't you c'mon over here and sit down on th' bed? Make yourself comfortable. [*She leads* ANNE *to the bed.*] How long you been livin' here, sugar?

ANNE: [*Still in shock*] Huh?

NANCY: I said, how long you been living here?

ANNE: I don't know.

THIS BIRD OF DAWNING | 125

NANCY: You don't know?

ANNE: Since my sis— About three and a half years. No—about one year.

NANCY: Ain't you sure?

ANNE: I lived in the apartment downstairs for two and a half years. Then a year ago I moved into this one.

NANCY: Yes'm, I sure do like this apartment. Ain't never been in no apartment like this befo'. No, ma'm, I ain't. [At door] Is this here yo'r bathroom?

ANNE: My bathroom?

NANCY: I wants to use th' toilet.

ANNE: No, you can't use my bathroom.

NANCY: Why can't I?

ANNE: It's out of order!

NANCY: Out of order?

ANNE: Yes!

NANCY: What do you do?

ANNE: In the basement—there's one in the basement.

NANCY: Basement?

ANNE: Next to the laundry room.

NANCY: Is that th' one you use?

ANNE: Yes.

NANCY: Y'mean t' tell me that ev'ry time you have to answer th' call of nature in th' middle of th' night, you hafta get up and go plum down int' th' basement?

ANNE: Yes, when my bathroom is out of order.

NANCY: Lord, have mercy, Jesus! Girl livin' in this fancy apartment an' havin' to get up an go t' th' basement to answer th' call of nature. Who else uses that bathroom?

ANNE: Well, it's for the people who work here.

NANCY: Y' mean th' servants?

ANNE: It's for everybody.

NANCY: You send all your guests down there?

ANNE: Yes.

NANCY: You mean to tell me when yo'r friends visit you, they all haffta go troopin' down int' th' cellar?

ANNE: It's a lovely bathroom, really it is. It's much nicer than my bathroom. As a matter of fact, I'd much rather use it than mine. It's really beautiful. It's a pleasure—an absolute joy to use. It's done with bright blue tiles on the floor with silver dollars in them. With walls of blond oakwood that are bright as a mirror. Bright enough to see your image in. And a ceiling with chandeliers hanging down filled with all kinds of colored lights. And a toilet seat made of ivory covered by a soft red cushion. It has a built-in perfume spray that comes on every seven minutes. And in the summer it has air conditioning. The winter electric heat . . .

NANCY: How'd I get to it?

ANNE: You take the elevator out there in the hall. You know the elevator out there in the hall? Well, you get into the elevator and you push the bottom button marked "B." B's for basement. It's the first one on the row on your right as you go into the elevator. You can't miss it. I think it's red. Yes, it's red. You can't miss it because it's red. The rest of the buttons are black, but it's red. Just punch it—press it. When you come out of the elevator you walk straight down the hall until you come to a wall. It's a wall painted red with a black stripe. You follow the red wall with the black stripe seven steps until you come to a door with the word "washroom" on it. Next to the washroom is a big red door. That's it.

NANCY: Suppose it's locked.

ANNE: It's not locked. They keep it open all the time.

NANCY: You mean to tell me that bathroom door is kept unlocked all day an' night?

ANNE: Yes.

NANCY: Well, I sure ain't, Lord, goin' down prowlin' 'round in that basement. Ain't no tellin' what might be lurkin' round down there in th' darkness. Justa waitin' for somebody t' come along so he can hit 'em in th' head.

ANNE: [*Tries to joke*] Don't be silly, there's no one down there.

NANCY: Why don't you c'mon down there with me?

ANNE: No—I'll wait here until you come back.

NANCY: [*Crossing to bathroom*] Well . . .

ANNE: Where're you going?

NANCY: See if it's still outta order. [*Exits into bathroom*]

ANNE: [*Furious*] Come out of there. [*Pounds on door*] Come out of there at once, do you hear me? [*Becoming hysterical*] I don't want you to use my bathroom. It's

my bathroom. You have no right to use it if I don't
want you to. What're you doing in there?

NANCY: [*Through the door*] I'm peein', what'd y' think I'm
doin'?

ANNE: Come out! You come out of my bathroom!

NANCY: [*Opening the door*] Is you done lost your mind, girl?
Screamin' n' hollerin' like that.

ANNE: Did you use it?

NANCY: [*Laughs*] Heeee! [*Points at her and continues to
laugh*]

ANNE: What're you laughing at, you hyena?

NANCY: Y' nightgown's wet.

ANNE: [*Feeling the wetness of gown*] Oh . . .

NANCY: Girl, you done stood up here and peed all over yo'rself.

ANNE: Shut up! [*Pulling nightgown from skin*]

NANCY: Yo'r bathroom ain't outta order.

ANNE: [*Takes a fresh gown from closet*] I'll have it extermi-
nated! [*Exits into bathroom*]

NANCY: You got roaches. [*She moves to whiskey cabinet and
picks up a bottle.*]

ANNE: [*Enters*] Put that down! [*Snatches bottle*]

NANCY: Look like you would offer me a little taste.

ANNE: I'll give you a drink and you'll go, all right?

NANCY: What'cha lookin' for?

ANNE: I had some paper cups around here someplace.

NANCY: Paper cup? I don't wanna drink outta no paper cup.
How come you can't give me a glass to drink out of?

ANNE: What difference does it make?

NANCY: [*Grinning*] If'n it doesn't make no diff'ence, can't I's
have it in a glass, Miss Anne, honey?

ANNE: Just another glass I have to wash.

NANCY: Don't y' has a colored gal to do that kinda work?

ANNE: No.

NANCY: [*Takes glass from shelf*] I'll wash th' glass. Sho' is a
beautiful glass. Just sparkles like brand-new money.
All dese pretty little designs. Reminds me of when
we were children. Awaking in the middle of the
night and seeing the windows of our room frozen. You
remember that, don't you, Anne?

ANNE: [*Pours her a drink*] Yes . . . No!

NANCY: [*After a pause*] Bet things sho' taste a lot mo' better outta a glass like this. [*Holds a glass up to light*] Now, ain't that pretty? Ain't never drinked nutthin' dis pretty befo'. I done drinked 'bout much as anybody in this world, I reckon. But I ain't done never drinked nuthin' dis pretty. [*Drinks it slowly*] It sho' taste better when you drink it from a pretty glass.

ANNE: You can have the glass.

NANCY: No'm. Couldn't do that. Break up yo'r set.

ANNE: It's all right, you can take the glass with you.

NANCY: Somethin' wrong with th' glass?

ANNE: No.

NANCY: Then why don't you wanna it no more?

ANNE: Thought you'd like to have it. You can always carry it with you—to drink out of.

NANCY: Wouldn't do me no good. Wouldn't be pretty where I go to drink. Gotta have somethin' nice 'round it—reflect on it. Like one of them magic mirrors. So ugly where I go t' drink. [*Hands glass to* ANNE, *who lets it smash on the floor*] Look at what you done done. [NANCY *bends down to pick up the pieces.* ANNE *stands over her, her hand around the neck of the bottle.*] Maybe you can glue it back together. [*She rises and hands the pieces to* ANNE. ANNE *takes the pieces and moves to the kitchen.*] Sure am sorry about your glass.

ANNE: You'll go now, won't you please?

NANCY: Oh, Lawdy, my feets is sho' killin' me.

ANNE: You said you'd leave.

NANCY: Lawd, dese heah tennis shoes is 'bout t' kill my po' feet. Youh ever wear tennis shoes, sugar? Dey sho' don't take no hard wearin', does dey?

ANNE: I think I have a pair of shoes I can let you have. [*She moves across to bedroom section to closet.*] I think . . . [*Finds a pair of shoes*] I was going to throw them out. Here.

NANCY: [*Examines them*] Sho' done been worn, ain't dey? See why youh wuz gwine throw 'em out. Lawd, dey just about worn out. Holes comin' in de soles.

ANNE: They're better than the ones you're wearing now.

NANCY: Yes, ma'm, dey sho' is, but dey done took on de characteristics of yo' foots. An' by de time my feets adjust t' de characteristics of yo' feets, my feets be squeezed into mush. 'Cause it is a hurtin' thing when y' haffta force yo' feets int' de characteristics of somebody else's feets. Now, I sho' don't wants ya t' think I ain't grateful t' ya fer givin' me dese heah ole worn-out shoes. Even if dey don't happen t' follow th' lines n' shape of my bunions 'n' corns. 'Course, now, dat ain't yo' fault. An' my feets is almost on de ground. But I did promise my foots that I never would wear no shoes behind nobody else, no mo'. Woman gave me a pair of shoes once an' y' know what? I picked up a fungus of de foot. Now, I dunno whether or not youh ever had a fungus of de feet. But I sho' wanna tell y' it is an aggravatin' thing to be plagued wit'. 'Course, now, I ain't sayin' that I suspicions youh'd might be a carrier of the plague of fungus of de foot. No, ma'm, I ain't sayin' that, atall, Miss Anne, honey. But on de other hand foot fungus is a very deceitful thing. Youh could have it 'n' not even know nuthin' 'bout it. 'Cause dem little things is clever. Bury demselves neath de skin an' hatch dey're eggs. Lawd? [*Picks up a pair of red shoes*] Sho' is some pretty shoes. Betcha youh sho' look good struttin' down de streets in dem red shoes. Sho' betcha ain't nobody looks as good as youh does when youh put on dese red shoes. Lawd, one thing I always did want was a pair of red shoes.

ANNE: [*Snatches shoes*] Give me those!

NANCY: Look brand-new!

ANNE: I've never worn them.

NANCY: Youh mean to tell me youh got dem shoes sittin' up heah in yo' closet n' ain't never even much worn dem?

ANNE: [*Clutching them*] I'm waiting for a special occasion.

NANCY: [*Touches shoes*] Sho' wished I could git me some red shoes.

ANNE: No! You can't have them!

NANCY: I ain't gwine take 'em from youh, Miss Anne, honey.

ANNE: I paid fifty dollars for these shoes!

NANCY: Whew! Fifty dollars for one pair of shoes!

ANNE: I had them specially made. Handmade. Measured to my feet.

NANCY: Sho', Lawd, wished I had me a pair of fifty-dollar red shoes . . . handmade t' fit de characteristics of my feets. Wonder if dey would fit m' feets? [*Snatches shoes*]

ANNE: [*Frightened*] What're you doing?

NANCY: [*Measuring shoe against her foot*] Just wanna measure yo' shoe 'gainst my feet. Well, sir, same size—exact same size. Ain't got no characteristics cut int' de leather.

ANNE: Your heel, it's too big!

NANCY: Ain't no bigger than yourn.

ANNE: Yes . . . it's . . . it's bigger—stronger than mine. It'll bust right through the back of the shoe.

NANCY: Well, if my heel is so strong, why did dem little cloth tennis shoes hurt it so much? I'm gonna try 'em on.

ANNE: No! Please . . . no.

NANCY: My feets is clean. [*Tries on shoes, walks about in them. She crosses into living room with* ANNE *following her.*] Sho' feels good on m' feet.

ANNE: Would you please take them off, before it's too late.

NANCY: Miss Anne, youh like entertainment?

ANNE: What?

NANCY: Betcha y' didn't know I could dance, did y'? 'Course I ain't never took no lessons or nuthin' like that. No, sir. Dancin' 'n' singin' just comes natural t' me. Might say I got natural-born rhythm. [*Takes* ANNE'*s hands and starts her clapping together*]
De camp town ladies sing dis song
Dew da
De camp town races five miles long
Oh, dew da day.
Now just keep this rhythm, Miss Anne. Don't stop now—don't stop! [ANNE *becomes caught up in the clapping as she watches* NANCY *sing and dance. Tap dancing.*]
Oh, de camp town ladies sing dis song
Dew da, dew da
De camp town races five miles long
Dew da, dew da
I came down heah wit' m' pocket full of tin
Dew da, dew da.

ANNE: [*Caught up*] You people sure are happy, aren't you? Why're you so happy, gal?

NANCY: [*Dancing to the rhythm of* ANNE's *clapping*] Miss
            Anne, honey, if you wuz ever a nigger for one Satur-
            day night, you'd never wanna be white no mor' long
            as you lived.
ANNE: Keep singing, gal.
NANCY: Gwine t' run all night, gwine t' run all day,
            I'll bet my money on de bobtail nag
            Somebody bet on de bay.
ANNE: Keep on singin', nigger gal.
NANCY: Heeee! Yes'm, Miss Anne.
ANNE: Why is it all you nigger gals got bad feet?
NANCY: Comes from wearin' all yo' ole shoes, Miss Anne
            ma'm.
ANNE: You're slowing down, nigger gal.
NANCY: Can't dance like I use to. Lawd. I sho' usta could
            dance. 'Member when I usta go downtown shoppin'
            . . . Usta dance for de folks that owned de store. Dey
            loved my stuff so much dey just usta up an' gimme
            dey're stuff for nuthin'.
ANNE: [*Still clapping*] Dance, nigger gal, dance!
NANCY: De camp town ladies sings dis song
            Dew da, dew da
            De camp town races track fives miles long
            De da, dew da.

            I came down here wit' my pockets full of tin
            Dew da, dew da
            I came down heah wit' my pockets full of tin
            Oh, dew da day.

            Gwine to run all night
            Gwine to run all day
            Bet my money on de bobtail nag
            Somebody bet on de bay.
            [*She stops.*] Now, you gotta dance for me, Miss Anne,
            honey.
ANNE: No, I can't.
NANCY: [*Pulls her knife*] Yes, you can.
ANNE: [*Frightened, starts to dance*] I can't . . .
NANCY: [*Clapping*] Sing, white gal, sing.
ANNE: De camp town ladies sings this song

Dew da, dew da
De camp town races sings this song
Dew da, dew da.

NANCY: You sings right nice for a white lady.

ANNE: [*Tiring*]
Gwine to run all night
Gwine to run all . . .
[*Trying to catch breath*]
I came down heah with my pockets full of tin
Oh . . . oh, dew da . . . day.

NANCY: Youh doin' fine, Miss Anne, honey.

ANNE: [*Still dancing*] I can't remember the words. [*Stops*]
Can't do it any more.

NANCY: Yes, you can.

ANNE: My arms—my arms hurt.

NANCY: Yo' arms hurt, sugar?

ANNE: Please, let me rest.

NANCY: Just one more minute.

ANNE: I can't keep the rhythm.

NANCY: That's cause yo' rhythm ain't natural.

ANNE: [*Collapses on floor*] You can have them!

NANCY: Huh?

ANNE: You can keep the shoes.

NANCY: Y' mean—youh is givin' me yo' shoes?

ANNE: Yes.

NANCY: Youh is such a sweet thing, y'know that? Anybody
ever tell youh that?

ANNE: My legs ache.

NANCY: Yo' legs ache, sugar?

ANNE: [*Crying*] Yes!

NANCY: [*Helping her up*] Well, youh jes' c'mere t' mammy.
[*Leads her to dining-room section.* NANCY *sits her on
her lap and begins rocking her.*] I's gwine mak' dat
ole devilish pain go way. Now, youh go way, Mister
Pain, 'n' leav' dis child alone. Y'heah me, Mister Pain?
Y' take yo' ole devilish self on way from 'round dis
child. [*Rocking*]
Mammy's little baby loves shorten' bread
Mammy's little baby loves shorten' bread . . .
Feelin' any better, honey lamb?

ANNE: [*Reluctantly*] Yes.

NANCY: Tole you Mammy would make dat ole devilish pain go way.

ANNE: It's all gone.

NANCY: I'm a hard sister when some kinda mean ole pain is tryin' to hurt m' little sweet lamb.

ANNE: You feel so soft and warm . . .

NANCY: Mammy's little baby loves shorten' bread
Mammy's little baby loves shorten' bread . . .

ANNE: I could just close my eyes and go right to sleep . . .

NANCY: [Humming] Dat right, you just go right on t' sleep.

ANNE: Your body is so warm . . .

NANCY: [Humming] Uhmm.

ANNE: Lenny Redmond's body was always so cold . . .

NANCY: Dat's dat ole no-count man youh wuz foolin' round with?

ANNE: His body was ice cold. Yours is like a furnace.

NANCY: Is you hungry, child?

ANNE: Yes.

NANCY: How 'bout a little ninny pie?

ANNE: Yes . . .

[NANCY arranges her blouse and ANNE buries her head in her chest as if being nursed.]

NANCY: Dat's right, honey—youh jest eat all youh wants to.
Mammy's little baby loves shorten' bread
Mammy's little baby loves shorten' bread . . .
Youh sho' is a hungry baby, ain't y'? Sho' is. Is dat ninny pie good t' der baby? [ANNE bites her. Pushing her away.] What did you do that for? Why'd you bite me?

ANNE: Don't take it away! Please, give it back to me.

NANCY: So you can bite it off th' next time!

ANNE: Why did you take it away from me?

NANCY: 'Cause youh didn't know how t' treat it.

ANNE: You mean ole thing.

NANCY: Next time maybe you'll know how to treat it.

ANNE: If I can't have it, then you get out of here!

NANCY: Get out?

ANNE: Right now.

NANCY: Where would I be goin' out in th' cold night?

ANNE: I don't give a damn where in the hell you go.

NANCY: Well, I do. You invited me here an' here is where I'm gonna stay.

ANNE: No, you're not.

NANCY: How we gonna do business if I don't stay here?

ANNE: Business? What kind of business?

NANCY: Same business youh's is in.

ANNE: I'm not in any kind of business.

NANCY: Aw, hush, you don't have play like that wit' me, girl.

ANNE: What're you talking about?

NANCY: [*Looking around room*] You sure have got some nice things. Hope I does a whole heap of business so I can buy me some nice things.

ANNE: I worked for those things.

NANCY: [*Laughing*] I jes' bet you did.

ANNE: What do you mean by that?

NANCY: Nuthin'.

ANNE: You meant something. What was it?

NANCY: How many clients you got?

ANNE: Clients?

NANCY: We gonna divide yo' clients or is I gonna haffta git my own?

ANNE: What kind of clients?

NANCY: Youh don't haffta play with me, child. I knows all about life.

ANNE: I don't know what you're talkin' 'bout.

NANCY: About. You dropped the "A."

ANNE: Don't you dare correct my English!

NANCY: All right—go right on droppin' letters from words.

ANNE: I want to know what you think I am.

NANCY: Y'knows good n' well what youh is.

ANNE: Stop double-talking me.

NANCY: We gonna do right nice together in business. Give 'em a choice.

ANNE: Give who a choice?

NANCY: Yo' clients.

ANNE: You—what're you saying to me?

NANCY: Youh and me both know you didn't work to get all of this, did y'?

ANNE: You're a liar! I worked hard for everything I have.

NANCY:	Where's your job?
ANNE:	My job?
NANCY:	Girl, you ain't never worked an' got all this. I been workin' all my natural-born life an' ain' near 'bout got this much.
ANNE:	You haven't been doing the right kind of work.
NANCY:	That's why I want to go into business with you.
ANNE:	You damn crazy black bitch, I keep telling you I'm not in business.
NANCY:	Your arrangements then. Now, what's the deal, commission or percentage?
ANNE:	Commissions or percentages?
NANCY:	Did you buy all these pretty things?
ANNE:	What are you talking about now?
NANCY:	Jes' askin' you if you bought all these pretty things?
ANNE:	None of your damn business!
NANCY:	How'd you get 'em then?
ANNE:	They were presents.
NANCY:	What's folks doin' givin' you all these presents?
ANNE:	None of your business!
NANCY:	What did you haffta do t' get all these presents?
ANNE:	Stop questioning me.
NANCY:	Ain't nobody ever gave me no presents for nuthin'. [NANCY *takes out a coat from the closet.*] You sure got some nice friends, ain't y'?
ANNE:	Give me my coat! [*Snatches it*]
NANCY:	I ain't gonna hurt it none.
ANNE:	And leave my things alone.
NANCY:	Jes' tryin' t' find out what y' haffta t' do t' get presents like this.
ANNE:	You go to hell!
NANCY:	Ain't you gonna let your sister in on the secret?
ANNE:	I've got no secrets!
NANCY:	Youh ain't scared of a little competition, are you?
ANNE:	From you? [*She laughs.*]
NANCY:	What you laughin' at?
ANNE:	[*Still laughing*] You competing with me?
NANCY:	That makes you laugh, huh? Think it's funny?
ANNE:	The only way you could compete with me would be in the alley.
NANCY:	Why don't you let your clients decide that?

ANNE:	They wouldn't spit on you!
NANCY:	Then you do have clients?
ANNE:	I didn't say that!
NANCY:	Then how do you know they wouldn't spit on me?
ANNE:	Because they don't deal with fifty-cent whores.
NANCY:	Just high-class whores like you.
ANNE:	I'm not a whore! I don't stand on the streets waiting for tricks.
NANCY:	That's exactly why I want to go into business with you. Sure get tired of standing on the streets.
ANNE:	That's where you belong! Standing on the streets, flagging cars passing by. You wouldn't even know how to . . .
NANCY:	You can teach me!
ANNE:	Teach you?
NANCY:	Yes'm, I'd be a good student, too.
ANNE:	[*After a pause*] Tell you what. Suppose you got a room somewhere? Once and a while I might send you a client.
NANCY:	What kind of client?
ANNE:	Clients that want some kind of special—kicks.
NANCY:	Naw, I don't like all that kind of funny business. I want good wholesome business. Nice, clean-cut clients.
ANNE:	Then get your own.
NANCY:	Y' mean you don't wanna share your clients with me?
ANNE:	It's not me. I just know they wouldn't accept you, that's all.
NANCY:	Why don't we give it a try for a while?
ANNE:	You'd ruin my business.
NANCY:	[*Pulls knife again*] You don't share your business with me, Sister, you ain't gonna be in business.
ANNE:	Don't threaten me.
NANCY:	I'll carve that white skin right off your face. Peel you like you was an apple.
ANNE:	I'll have you arrested.
NANCY:	Nobody would know if you was black or white. Just peel all the skin off your face.
ANNE:	Don't hurt me! Please, don't hurt me.
NANCY:	Wonder what dirty word would they call somebody with no skin.
ANNE:	Stay away from me.

NANCY: That's all you got, ain't it? That white skin . . .
ANNE: You can't frighten me! I'm not afraid of you, you dirty stinking nigger!
NANCY: I'm gonna peel you.
ANNE: [*Suddenly*] All right! I'll take you in.
NANCY: No, you won't! Invite me here, then try t' put me out on t' street. Just better go on an' do you in.
ANNE: You wouldn't kill your own sister, would you?
NANCY: But you said we were no kin.
ANNE: [*Moving to letters on floor*] Didn't I write you all these letters? [*Picking up some of the letters*] Didn't I tell you about all my dreams and hopes for both of us?
NANCY: But you said they weren't for me. Said you didn't address them to me. Wasn't even meant for me to read.
ANNE: Yes they were . . .
NANCY: Trying to play some kinda trick on me.
ANNE: No, I'm not, Nancy . . . honey.
NANCY: I oughta cut your lying heart out.
ANNE: You wouldn't hurt me—your own sister. Your own flesh and blood.
NANCY: Just think I'm so dumb you can tell me anything and I'll believe it, d'y?
ANNE: I don't believe you'd hurt me. I just don't believe you could bring yourself to hurt me.
NANCY: You don't, huh?
ANNE: No, I don't. [*Pause*] Oh, Sister, you don't know how happy I am to have you here with me, at last. I need you.
NANCY: Need me for what?
ANNE: Remember I told you I had a bad heart? I shouldn't live here alone—by myself.
NANCY: Yea.
ANNE: I . . . I need a friend. A sister. My health is on the verge of total collapse. Sometimes I think . . . I get frightened about my having a heart attack here alone. I want you to come and live with me. Would you do that for me? I know it may not be too much fun for you having to look after an invalid.
NANCY: You want me to come and live here with you? Here in this apartment? [*Pause*] Want me to come an' work for you? Be your maid?

ANNE:	I want you to come here and live with me as my sister.
NANCY:	How could you be kin to something like me?
ANNE:	Will you do me this favor?
NANCY:	Now, I don't know. This complaint you got—is it contagious?
ANNE:	Heart disease isn't contagious.
NANCY:	Sure don't want to catch nothin'.
ANNE:	You won't catch anything.
NANCY:	Can't be too careful 'bout your health, y'know. An' this apartment ain't big enough for two people.
ANNE:	Maybe we might move into one of the larger apartments in the building.
NANCY:	Got to be getting up in the middle of the night. Go trampin' down in that basement to squeeze my kidneys an' other muscles.
ANNE:	But the bathroom isn't out of order any more.
NANCY:	Mean you don't mind me using your bathroom?
ANNE:	You're my sister, aren't you?
NANCY:	You gonna pee on yourself every time I use your bathroom?
ANNE:	Oh, please, don't embarrass me about that, Sister.
NANCY:	Wouldn't want you ruinin' all your nightgowns.
ANNE:	I just got excited.
NANCY:	I won't have to go downstairs to the bathroom?
ANNE:	Certainly not. You think I'd send my sister all the way down into that dirty, filthy basement? Through those dark halls where someone might be lurking to hurt her.
NANCY:	Can I keep the red shoes?
ANNE:	I gave them to you, didn't I?
NANCY:	Can I have my name on the mailbox?
ANNE:	Sure, you can. And every day I'll write you a letter. And I'll mail it right here to you. Write your name on it with this address on it . . . and the mailman will deliver it right here to you. He'll see your name on the mailbox right next to mine. I'll give you a key and you go down every day and open the mailbox and collect your letters.
NANCY:	I ain't got nobody to write to me.
ANNE:	Yes, you have.
NANCY:	Folks don't write to me.

ANNE: Don't be silly.

NANCY: Watched many a mailman pass me by.

ANNE: I'll write you letters.

NANCY: Like you did when I lived down in Elan?

ANNE: Every day I'll write you a letter.

NANCY: Put my name on it and mail it to me?

ANNE: Every day.

NANCY: You're lying to me!

ANNE: I love you, Nancy.

NANCY: No, you don't. You hate me.

ANNE: Oh, my poor, sweet Sister. You've been so hurt, haven't you?

NANCY: Get away from me. Don't you come near me.

ANNE: Give me the knife, Sister dear.

NANCY: Aw naw . . .

ANNE: Then put the knife away, honey.

[*Slowly* NANCY *puts the knife in her pocket. The two women stand facing each other*.]

NANCY: You ain't foolin' me, are y'? You ain't playin' some kinda trick on me?

ANNE: [*Touches her*] Sister . . .

NANCY: [*Deeply touched*] Sister!

ANNE: [*Moves to bar*] I'm going to fix myself a drink. [*She pours herself a drink, crosses to closet.*]

NANCY: Where're you going, Sister dear?

ANNE: I'm going to get a nightgown. Thought you might be tired and want to go to bed.

NANCY: Where am I going to sleep? Out here on the couch?

ANNE: [*Lays gown on bed*] You'll sleep in my bed.

NANCY: Where will you sleep?

ANNE: In my bed. [*She points the gown out to her, then brings it to her for inspection.*] I thought you might like this to sleep in. It's brand-new—never been worn.

NANCY: [*Touching it*] Sure is thin. Catch your death of cold in something this thin. [*Runs her hands across it*] I ain't never slept in no nightgown before. Always slept in my underwear.

ANNE: Why don't you go into the bathroom and put it on?

NANCY: I'd feel foolish sleeping in this tissue-paper thing. [*Touching it again*] Sure feels soft, huh?

ANNE:	Feels wonderful on the body, too.
NANCY:	Does?
ANNE:	[*Rubs it across* NANCY's *face*] Soft as a cloud. Why don't you go into the bathroom and undress—put it on?
NANCY:	Aw, I can undress right here, I ain't shame-face!
ANNE:	Don't you want to wash up?
NANCY:	I already washed today.
ANNE:	But you'll feel better if you wash up before bed.
NANCY:	I generally wash up in the morning when I get up.
ANNE:	What's wrong, don't you trust me, Sister dear?
NANCY:	Aw, I trust you, Sister.
ANNE:	Aren't you going to take off your coat?
NANCY:	Yea, guess I better. [*She slips out of her coat and lays it on the bed. She disappears into bathroom.*]

[ANNE *stands staring down at coat until she hears the water begin to run. She seizes the coat and throws it to floor. She removes the knife from* NANCY's *pocket and hides it under one of the pillows on the bed.*]

ANNE:	Sister!
NANCY:	[*Off stage*] Huh?
ANNE:	You know what I'd like, Sister?
NANCY:	[*Off stage. Over water*] What's that?
ANNE:	[*Getting two glasses and whiskey from bar*] Take the little glass over the basin and bring me a little water. [*She takes several pills from one of bottles and slips them into the glass and fills both glasses with whiskey.*]
NANCY:	[*Enters with a glass of water*] Here. [*Sets glass down on table next to bed*]
ANNE:	I'll fix you a drink. [*She pours a little of the water into her whiskey glass.*]
NANCY:	Is this mine?
ANNE:	I always have a little drink before I go to bed. You don't have to. It makes me sleep a little better.
NANCY:	[*Tasting*] Taste funny!
ANNE:	Don't drink it then. [*She moves and sits on side of bed with knife under pillow.*]
NANCY:	Drunk so much of this ole bad whiskey. Good whiskey —ain't used to. [*She takes a long swallow, then another. Finally finishes it, climbing into bed.* ANNE *leaps up off the bed.*] Ain't you coming to bed?

THIS BIRD OF DAWNING | 141

ANNE:	[*Sits in chair near bed*] In a moment.
NANCY:	You'd better c'mon to bed, Sister.
ANNE:	In a little while.
NANCY:	Now, you c'mon to bed. Do you hear me?
ANNE:	Yes, I hear you.
NANCY:	Well, Lord—sure didn't know I was this tired. [*Relaxing in bed*] Feel like I'm just floating away.
ANNE:	[*Moves to bed*] You need rest.
NANCY:	Feel dizzy in my head. Bed feels like it's spinnin'!
ANNE:	[*Sitting down on bed*] I'll keep it still for you.
NANCY:	No need for you to stay up half th' night on my account. [*Falls asleep*]
ANNE:	Sister? . . . Sister? [*Shakes her softly*] Sister? [*She slips knife from under pillow, plunges knife into* NANCY *several times.*] Die! You stinking black bitch! [*Pulls* NANCY's *body out of bed onto floor*] Get out of my bed, you dirty, filthy black bitch! [*Suddenly she clutches her heart. She drops knife and moves to table. She falls on table, knocking over the bottles, which break on floor. She crawls to telephone and tries to call on the damaged phone. She collapses to floor.*] Oh, my God, help me. Don't let me die! Please, don't let me die! [*She crawls to* NANCY's *body.*] Help me, please, help me! [*She tries to blow her breath into* NANCY's *mouth.*] Wake up! Why don't you wake up and help me! Wake up! Do you hear me, you black bitch! Get up, do you hear? Get up and get me some help, gal! [*Pause*] I'm sorry. Please, help me, Nancy. [*Another pause*] You don't want to help me, do you? You want me to die! I'll let you stay, I promise I will. You can have anything you want. I'll give you anything you want—just get me a doctor. My doctor is named Hunt Gray. Dr. Hunt Gray. You can find him listed in the telephone book. Tell him to hurry. I feel like I've been hit by a truck. [*A light rises on* ANNE, *turning her skin black.*] C'mon dere, gal, an' git up on y' feet. Youh heah me, Miss Nancy? Youh better hurry up dere, gal, ifin you gwine help me. Youh doesn't want me t' die, does youh? Oh, Lawdy, have mercy, Jesus. Mercy! Jesus, Mercy! [*Sees her hand*] Lawd, my hand is black. Oh, Lawdy, Jesus, don't let me lay

up heah an' die de death of a nigger. Youh can't do dat t' me, 'cause I is white. I ain't suppose t' die like dis. I ain't gwine die de death of a nigger! I's gwine die a white woman. Yes, suh, I's white. If I can't die de death of a white woman, I ain't gonna die at all. [*Tries to crawl toward the door*] Gotta get outta heah. Dey ain't gwine find me in heah wit' dat gal. Folk ain't gonna be able t' tell which is which. [*She reaches up for the doorknob and the stage begins to fade into darkness. She loses the grip on door and the hand falls off the knob. The last thin light fades and the stage is in total blackout. Curtain.*]

THE MINSTREL BOY

The lights come up on an apartment in Harlem about two o'clock in the morning. The apartment is in a state of semidarkness. The living room is at left stage with the entrance in the down left wall. The kitchen is at right stage with a small door for the bathroom on the down right wall. Between the kitchen and the living room is a small bedroom, up stage center. The wall has been cut away so that we may view the interior of the bedroom. The set should not be realistic but should suggest something that is viewed as in a dream. In other words, it should have a certain liquid quality about it.

The door opens and RAINBOW RIVERS enters. He is a small man with a deep-hue black skin and between fifty-five and sixty years old, dressed in a pair of powdered trousers, red vest over a canary shirt, green shoes and a purple felt hat. He carries a long staff with an orange canvas bag attached to the end of it. He moves across the dark stage, making his way into the kitchen. He snaps on the light and lays his bag on the table. He moves to the bathroom and gets a bottle of alcohol. He rolls up his pants leg to reveal a dirty rag tied around his leg. He pours some of the alcohol on his leg and groans.

From the bedroom we hear the sound of CAY crying out in her sleep. At first RAINBOW freezes and just listens.

RAINBOW: [Limping to the edge of kitchen] Cay? [She is still crying in her sleep.] Cay!
CAYELLA: [Suddenly awakening] Rainbow!
RAINBOW: You was havin' a nightmare. Better go back to sleep.
CAYELLA: Rainbow? [She rises, gets out of bed. She is a strong-looking woman about the same age and color as RAINBOW.] Rainbow? [She comes into kitchen wiping her eyes.]

RAINBOW: What'd you cryin' about?

CAYELLA: Musta been cryin' in my sleep.

RAINBOW: What was you cryin' about in your sleep?

CAYELLA: I don't remember. . . . Maybe I ain't cryin' at all. Maybe my eyes are just watering from my sinuses.

RAINBOW: Go to bed upset about somethin'?

CAYELLA: What happened to your leg?

RAINBOW: Got bitten. Would you hand me some of that cotton out of the bathroom, please?

CAYELLA: [*Getting cotton*] How did you get bitten?

RAINBOW: [*Taking cotton*] Crazy young gal bite me right in the fat part of my leg. Felt like she was gonna tear the muscle right out.

CAYELLA: Where were you when she bite you?

RAINBOW: On the stage. Climbed right up on the stage and almost took a hunk outta my leg.

CAYELLA: [*Looking at wound*] Lord, have mercy. [*Moves to bathroom and returns with a jar of dirt. She moves to sink, pours some dirt into saucer, then mixes it with water. She moves back to* RAINBOW.] Let me put some of this on it.

RAINBOW: You crazy? Get outta here with that dirt.

CAYELLA: It's got healin' powers in it.

RAINBOW: Healin' powers? That ain't nothin' but mud.

CAYELLA: It's earth and woman raised to the seventh power. Spiritualist woman give it to me for my skin. She put healin' powers in it.

RAINBOW: Won't use those creams the skin doctor gave you. After all the money I paid out to skin doctors, you foolin' round with th' spiritualist.

CAYELLA: She says I got alligator skin.

RAINBOW: I don't wanna hear none of that mess.

CAYELLA: She says I have to keep rubbing down with the mud . . . until . . .

RAINBOW: Until what?

CAYELLA: Until the alligator skin commence to fall away.

RAINBOW: Both you fools oughta be put away—locked up.

CAYELLA: It's your fault . . . that I have been afflicted with alligator skin.

RAINBOW: [*Standing up*] I told you I don't want to hear none of your foolishness.

CAYELLA: Your actions brought on my affliction.

RAINBOW: Woman, will you go to bed and go to sleep, please, ma'm.

CAYELLA: So I can continue to have bad nightmares.

RAINBOW: Then I'm going to bed. [*He starts for bedroom.*]

CAYELLA: She told me you'd be home tonight.

RAINBOW: Th' spiritualist woman?

CAYELLA: Said you'd come home tonight from Philadelphia.

RAINBOW: How did she know that?

CAYELLA: Woman's got second sight. How many times do I have to tell you that?

RAINBOW: She say anything else?

CAYELLA: I'd rather not say.

RAINBOW: [*Moves to table and sits down*] Did she tell you they would boo me?

CAYELLA: College students?

RAINBOW: Jitterbugs. Booin' me an' callin' me names. Tellin' me to get off the stage. Damn no-account jitterbugs!

CAYELLA: Probably college students.

RAINBOW: College students hell! Educated fools is more like it. Callin' me ignorant . . . [*Pause, full of pain*] I may not have much school learnin' but I sho' got enough mother wit to know how to act in public. And it's them same jitterbugs that's been followin' me around wherever I go. Is that what they're teachin' 'em in them schools—how'd stop folks from makin' an honest livin'?

CAYELLA: She said a blue-eyed devil with a golden crown would cause you to be wounded.

RAINBOW: Kingsley? Was she talkin' about Kingsley?

CAYELLA: She didn't call no names. Just said that the blue-eyed devil whose shadow you were would cause you to be wounded.

RAINBOW: She couldn't been talkin' 'bout Kingsley. No, sir! If Kingsley hadda been there, they never woulda treated me th' way they did, no, sir. If Kingsley was still in good health and we was doin' our act, they wouldn't've treated me like they did. [*Pause*] Know how they billed me? "The Extra Added Attraction." Thirty-five years in the business an' that's how they billed me. Put me way up on the fifth floor in a little dingy, dirty dressing room with a little yellow-stained face bowl with the hot-water faucet busted and no toilet. Had to walk all the way down to the basement to use the bathroom. Damn manager come askin' me why I kept a slop jar in my dressin' room. Told me it was against the rules of the health department to keep slop jars in the dressin' room. Threaten to break my contract on the grounds that I was a health menace. Stick me in a little dirty dressin' room without proper toilet facilities and then have the nerve to call me a health menace. Told him that I didn't have to put up with that kind of treatment. Must have thought I was the porter or somethin'. Had to let him know who I was! I use to get five hundred fan letters a week from all over the United States. Called by the critics a dusty Charlie Chaplin. Got featured billing in every one of Jerome Kingsley's movies. Now a little, rat-trap theater gonna bill me as an "Extra Added Attraction" and a little fifty-dollar-a-week fool is gonna tell me that I can't keep a slop jar in my dressin' room. In the old days I wouldn't have thought about settin' foot in a rat trap like that. An' that manager—I told him to keep them rowdy jitterbugs outta th' theater. But he didn't pay me no attention whatsoever. Well, I'll never work for him again, no, sir. He can call here— come up here and get down on his knees an' beg me an' I still wouldn't walk back into that theater. Hate to see any man lose his job, but if they want me to finish out the contract, they gonna have to get rid of him. [*Bangs table*] Had no business bookin' me in that theater in the first place. Told them in front they should try to book me on a Southern tour. [*Rises, gets a drink of water*] Always did have a big following in th' South. Ev'ry movie I ever made made a piss pot full of money outta th' South. Some theaters even much billed me over Kingsley in th' South. [*Pause*] Should still be out in Hollywood now —makin' that long money. Didn't just have to work with Kingsley. Coulda made my own pictures or been some other comedian's shadow. Some folks said it was me that made Kingsley a star. [*Pause, moves back to table*] Not one picture that I was in with Kingsley ever lost money. When he tried to make a picture without me it was a flop. We would have been together forever if it hadn't been for them nigger organizations puttin' th' pressure on him. Tellin' him that I was presentin' a bad image for Negroes. Didn't like it 'cause I rolled my eyes. Lots of white comedians roll their eyes and nobody says nothin' about it. But because I was a Negro I couldn't do it. I was givin' them good, clean comedy. But they didn't want that. They wanted the comedians that talked about race—race and more race. Insultin' th' audience an' bringin' up things folks don't wanna hear. That ain't comedy. Folks go t' see a show to forget their troubles. [*Pause*] I did a lot for Negroes out in Hollywood. I helped pave th' way for a lot of 'em that's makin' long money today. An' what's my pay? To be booed and bit in th' fat part of my leg—dragged off the stage and . . .

CAYELLA: And what, Rainbow?

RAINBOW: Nothin'!

CAYELLA: What did they do to you when they dragged you off the stage?

RAINBOW: Go ask the spiritual lady—she knows everything.

CAYELLA: Did they take you to a golden-haired, blue-eyed devil?

RAINBOW: Never mind where they took me.

CAYELLA: It was Kingsley they were after. They couldn't get to Kingsley, they took it out on you.

RAINBOW: Then what were they callin' my name for? What did they boo me for? Besides, Kingsley ain't never done them no harm. He built that beautiful hospital for 'em down South.

CAYELLA: What hospital?

RAINBOW: You know good 'n' well what hospital. The one he built outside of Jackson for just Negroes. Kingsley did a lot of good for all people.

CAYELLA: Lies. He tricked you into believing he built a hospital.

RAINBOW: I saw the hospital with my own eyes.

CAYELLA: He paid someone to cast a spell on you, make you believe that he had built a hospital. A hospital which you thought you saw with your own eyes.

RAINBOW: You better stay away from that spiritualist woman, 'cause she done drove you crazy. [*Pause*] How's he gonna put a spell on me?

CAYELLA: The night before you went to Philadelphia, he invited us over to his house for dinner—made us eat that strange food.

RAINBOW: That was health food. You know how Kingsley loves health food.

CAYELLA: That strange cheese he served us wrapped in figs and filled with some kind of strange grain . . .

RAINBOW: That was barley soup.

CAYELLA: And that bony-face little white dwarf sitting in the corner playing that strange music on the flute.

RAINBOW: He's been with Kingsley since we broke up.

CAYELLA: He was castin' a spell on you.

RAINBOW: Woman, will you get away from me with your old random talk, please, ma'm?

CAYELLA: An' th' other man?

RAINBOW: What other man?

CAYELLA: The skinny bony-face man with the bald head, dressed in a loose-fitting black suit . . .

RAINBOW: I don't remember nobody looking like that.

CAYELLA: He was sitting there in the corner next to the dwarf.

RAINBOW: If he was sitting there, how come I didn't see him?

CAYELLA: The spell must've been already on you.

RAINBOW: I didn't see anybody like that.

CAYELLA: Did you notice his shoes?

RAINBOW: Shoes—what about his shoes?

CAYELLA: The soles of his shoes. You could see the cuts in the leather. They were like cuts made from a shovel. They had a bit of dew on the tops of his shoes as if he had walked through a graveyard. Did Kingsley ever ask you whether or not you had a pair of old shoes?

RAINBOW: [*A little frightened*] What would Kingsley want with my old shoes?

CAYELLA: Would you rather be cremated or buried?

RAINBOW: [*Getting up from table and going into living room*] You shut up.

CAYELLA: I just want to know in case . . . [*She comes into living room.*] Rainbow? Rainbow!! Rainbow!!! Where is that good-for-nothing? [*She crosses into kitchen and gets his bag.*] What you doin' in my hen house, nigger? [*She picks up staff.*]

RAINBOW: [*Sitting on couch*] I don't feel like no playin', woman.

CAYELLA: [*Throws bag at him*] What you doin' in my hen house, nigger?

RAINBOW: I don't feel like no playin'.

CAYELLA: [*Hits him over head with stick*] I said, what you doin' in my hen house?

RAINBOW: [*Leaps to his feet*] Woman, you gone crazy! What th' matter with you? You done hit me in th' head!

CAYELLA: [*Aiming stick as if a rifle*] Who's in my chicken house? You'd better come on outta there with your hands up. Did you hear me? Who's in my chicken house?

RAINBOW: [*Frightened, drops to his knees and crawls under table*] Ain't nobody here but us chickens?

CAYELLA: Then you better start layin' some eggs.

RAINBOW: I'm alayin', missey—I'm alayin'! [*Takes black egg from bag and rolls it across floor*]

CAYELLA: Why is this egg so black?

RAINBOW: Look where they come from, heeheehee.

CAYELLA: C'mon outta there, you chicken thief.

RAINBOW: [*Still under table*] I ain't took nothin', boss lady.

CAYELLA: You better come on outta there. It's haunted under there.

RAINBOW: [*Frozen*] It's haunted under here. [*Pause*] Who's under here that ain't suppose t' be under here? [*Feeling for his feet*] Feets, is there somebody under here that ain't suppose to be? 'Cause if there is . . . feets, I want you to do your stuff.

CAYELLA: Ghosts are coming to get you, Rainbow.

RAINBOW: Feets, don't fail me now.

CAYELLA: Ghost gonna get you and take you away.

RAINBOW: Feets, will you c'mon?

CAYELLA: [*Sounding like a ghost*] Rainbow . . . Rainbow . . .

RAINBOW: What you want? What you callin' me fer?

CAYELLA: Why are you afraid, nigger?

RAINBOW: It ain't me that scared. It's my feets.

CAYELLA: Why are you sweatin', nigger?

RAINBOW: [*Wiping sweat off face*] That ain't sweat, Miss Ghost—that's ink.

CAYELLA: [*Pause*] Rainbow?

RAINBOW: Huh?

CAYELLA: What's that? Do you hear it?

RAINBOW: Hear what? I don't hear anything.

CAYELLA: You can't hear it? I can hear it.

RAINBOW: Hear what?

CAYELLA: Those students from Philadelphia.

RAINBOW: Them rowdy jitterbugs?

CAYELLA: They've followed you here—all the way from Philadelphia.

RAINBOW: I don't hear nothin'.

A MOB OF VOICES: [*In the distance*] We want Kingsley! We want Kingsley! We want Kingsley!

RAINBOW: It's them . . . it's them! [*Moves to window*] I don't see them.

CAYELLA: They must be hiding . . . out there.

RAINBOW: Where? Where are they hidin'?

MOB: We want Kingsley! We want Kingsley! We want Kingsley!

CAYELLA: They're callin' for you.

RAINBOW: They're not callin' me. They're callin' for Kingsley!

CAYELLA: You're his shadow—you'll have to go in his place.

RAINBOW: They already had me. I ain't gonna let them get me again.

CAYELLA: Go out and make them laugh. Turn all of their anger into laughter. That's what Kingsley would do.

RAINBOW: I tried to, but . . . they dragged me off the stage and took me away.

CAYELLA: Where did they take you, Rainbow?

RAINBOW: . . . to a field . . . in the middle of nowhere . . . where they filled my clothes with straw and put a blond wig on me. Then they tied me to a post . . . said I had a crooked spine. Then they beat me . . . spreaded my legs apart and brought branches from trees and beat my personal. Beat it until it was swollen and doubled up like the pipe under that face bowl in my dressing room . . . [*Sound of a flute is heard.*] Somebody was playing a flute . . . as

THE MINSTREL BOY | 153

they kept on beatin' me. I could feel my personal so heavy from the swellin' that it felt like it was gonna pull me down. Then they got hay and started a fire around me . . . not close enough to burn. Just close enough for me to feel the heat. [*Pause*] Then they put the fire out and untied me . . . laid me down on the ground. Then young girls came with a pail of soot and powdered my personal. They powdered my personal and my private parts with the black soot . . . [*The sound of the flute fades away along with the* MOB.] Then they were gone and I was alone in this big deserted field. Beside me was a can . . . I open the lid and it was ashes. And on the can, Kingsley's name was written . . . but scratched out. And underneath it was—mine? My name . . . Rainbow River written in where his had been scratched out.

CAYELLA: Scratched his name and written in yours. What else did they do?

RAINBOW: Did I say they did anything else!

CAYELLA: The woman told me.

RAINBOW: She told you . . . how when they took me down from the post . . . they . . .

CAYELLA: They what?

RAINBOW: My clothes were smokin' . . . they peed on me!

CAYELLA: You must have imagined it. Those kids wouldn't do a thing like that to you.

RAINBOW: They peed on me! And they're waitin' out there now.

CAYELLA: Who? Who's waiting where for you?

RAINBOW: Them rowdy jitterbugs!

CAYELLA: [*At window*] I don't see anyone.

RAINBOW: [*Coming to window*] They are not out there?

CAYELLA: Do you see anyone?

RAINBOW: Can't you hear them?

CAYELLA: I can't hear anything.

RAINBOW: You heard it first.

CAYELLA: I haven't heard anythin'.

RAINBOW: [*Moving to couch*] I best sit down . . . don't feel too well.

CAYELLA: You said this all took place in Philadelphia, didn't you?

RAINBOW: Yes, that's what I said.
CAYELLA: How could they follow you here from Philadelphia?
RAINBOW: I don't know.
CAYELLA: Maybe you imagined the whole thing.
RAINBOW: Imagined the whole thing?
CAYELLA: [*She crosses to bedroom.*] Rainbow?
RAINBOW: What do you want?
CAYELLA: [*Comes to couch carrying a doll dressed like a king*] Look what I have for you.
RAINBOW: What?
CAYELLA: [*Hands doll to him*] It's Kingsley.
RAINBOW: That woman . . .
CAYELLA: She made it from pictures of Kingsley.
RAINBOW: What'd you have this thing made up for?
CAYELLA: So you could hang it up and set fire to it.
RAINBOW: [*Throws it on floor*] You done lost your mind . . . or are you tryin' to make me lose mine?
CAYELLA: You will unless you free yourself from him. [*She moves to doll.*]
RAINBOW: I don't have to get free of anybody.
CAYELLA: Then you'll go crazy. You'll keep imaginin' that you've been tortured and peed on.
RAINBOW: I didn't imagine it. It happened.
CAYELLA: Destroy the doll and set us both free. I don't want to be married to a shadow.
RAINBOW: Why do you say that I imagine things?
CAYELLA: Hang it! Burn it!
RAINBOW: I don't want to do nobody no harm.
CAYELLA: [*Runs to bedroom and returns with another doll. It is an image of* RAINBOW] Either you destroy it or I'll . . .
RAINBOW: What's that?
CAYELLA: It's you, Minstrel Boy!
RAINBOW: Where'd you get that thing?
CAYELLA: Same place I got the other one.
RAINBOW: You give me that thing.
CAYELLA: Not until you destroy Kingsley.
RAINBOW: I ain't playin' with you!
CAYELLA: All right, you stupid nigger! [*She smashes it with her foot.*]
RAINBOW: [*Grabbing his head*] Stop it! [*Falls to floor*] Stop it!

THE MINSTREL BOY | 155

CAYELLA: On your knees, Minstrel Boy. Clown! Buffoon! Jester!

RAINBOW: You're stompin' my brains out!

CAYELLA: [*Still stomping doll*] I want to stomp them out.

RAINBOW: Stop, please stop.

CAYELLA: I gave you your chance.

RAINBOW: My head is splitting!

CAYELLA: Good! [*There is a pause. She falls back on couch. He, on his knees, remains still.*] You liked it, didn't you? You liked being dragged off that stage and carried out to the field to be beaten. Anything that kept you close to Kingsley.

RAINBOW: Why do you hate him so much?

CAYELLA: Because I wanted to see you free—your own man.

RAINBOW: You think I don't know?

CAYELLA: Know what?

RAINBOW: All the years you laid with him.

CAYELLA: You knew?

RAINBOW: Thought I was a fool, . . . didn't know what was goin' on.

CAYELLA: Why didn't you say anything?

RAINBOW: Because . . .

CAYELLA: Because you were going with his wife. Sniffin' around after her. Did you ever have her, Minstrel Boy?

RAINBOW: No.

CAYELLA: What would she want with the shadow of what she already had?

RAINBOW: Is that why you laid with him all these years?

CAYELLA: Why didn't you stop it? Once—just once why didn't you try and stop it? Didn't you care, Minstrel Boy?

RAINBOW: Stop callin' me Minstrel Boy!

CAYELLA: Why didn't you stop me?

RAINBOW: How? He paid my salary . . .

CAYELLA: And you shared your wife. [*Pause*] That's why I never had a child, y'know.

RAINBOW: Scared you wouldn't know which of us would be the father?

CAYELLA: I didn't want to reproduce either one of you.

RAINBOW: Is that why you always got rid of them?

CAYELLA: Yes.

RAINBOW: How many were there?

CAYELLA: I lost count . . . a long time ago.

RAINBOW: [*Rises with doll of Kingsley*] Kingsley . . .
CAYELLA: Maybe I destroyed the wrong doll. I kicked your doll to death. I could have gotten both of you if I had kicked his doll.

[*Pause*]

RAINBOW: Why didn't you?
CAYELLA: I wanted you to do it.
RAINBOW: [*Hands her the doll*] Still have your chance.
CAYELLA: [*Takes doll*] He's dead.
RAINBOW: Kingsley? Kingsley is dead?
CAYELLA: He shot himself this morning.
RAINBOW: You're lyin'.
CAYELLA: No—you know he's been sick for years. Found he had cancer. Mrs. Kingsley told me a long time ago. Didn't want you to know for fear you'd tell Kingsley.
RAINBOW: [*Grabs her by the throat*] You and the spiritualist woman did it!
CAYELLA: I didn't even know the spiritualist woman then—when he got it. She can't give cancer anyway.
RAINBOW: [*Lets her go*] Kingsley! Kingsley! Kingsley can't be dead. You can't die Kingsley . . . you can't die on me like this. Oh, God, why didn't you give it to me too? Why didn't you rot out my guts along with his? [*He crosses to bathroom with his bag and closes door.*]
CAYELLA: [*Moves to bathroom door*] Rainbow! [*She bangs on door.*] Rainbow! [*The sound of a body hitting against something is heard.* CAYELLA *enters the bathroom and the stage is empty for a moment. The sound of a telephone is heard ringing. She comes out of bathroom and crosses into bedroom.*] Hello, yes . . . he's home. He just hanged himself. He had come back from Philadelphia very depressed. Yes . . . yes. No, I don't want you to come over . . . Kingsley. He belongs to me now. Not you any more . . .

[*The lights fade.*]

THE MINSTREL BOY | 157